# STARFINDER

**Development Leads** • Jason Keeley and Owen K.C. Stephens
**Authors** • Stephen Radney-MacFarland, with Mikko Kallio,
   Jason Keeley, Lyz Liddell, Ron Lundeen, Mark Moreland,
   and Owen K.C. Stephens
**Cover Artist** • David Alvarez
**Interior Artists** • Taylor Fischer, Victor Manuel Leza Moreno,
   David Melvin, Mark Molnar, and Ainur Salimova
**Cartographer** • Damien Mammoliti

**Creative Directors** • James Jacobs, Robert G. McCreary,
   and Sarah E. Robinson
**Director of Game Design** • Jason Bulmahn
**Managing Developer** • Adam Daigle
**Development Coordinator** • Amanda Hamon Kunz
**Organized Play Lead Developer** • John Compton
**Developers** • Crystal Frasier, Jason Keeley, Ron Lundeen,
   Joe Pasini, Chris Sims, and Linda Zayas-Palmer
**Starfinder Design Lead** • Owen K.C. Stephens
**Starfinder Society Developer** • Thurston Hillman
**Senior Designer** • Stephen Radney-MacFarland
**Designers** • Logan Bonner and Mark Seifter
**Managing Editor** • Judy Bauer
**Senior Editor** • Christopher Carey
**Editors** • James Case, Lyz Liddell, Adrian Ng, and
   Lacy Pellazar
**Art Director** • Sonja Morris
**Senior Graphic Designers** • Emily Crowell and Adam Vick
**Franchise Manager** • Mark Moreland
**Project Manager** • Gabriel Waluconis

**Publisher** • Erik Mona
**Paizo CEO** • Lisa Stevens
**Chief Operations Officer** • Jeffrey Alvarez
**Chief Financial Officer** • John Parrish
**Chief Technical Officer** • Vic Wertz
**Director of Sales** • Pierce Watters
**Sales Associate** • Cosmo Eisele
**Vice President of Marketing & Licensing** • Jim Butler
**Marketing Manager** • Dan Tharp
**Licensing Manager** • Glenn Elliott
**Organized Play Manager** • Tonya Woldridge
**Accountant** • Christopher Caldwell
**Data Entry Clerk** • B. Scott Keim
**Director of Technology** • Dean Ludwig
**Web Production Manager** • Chris Lambertz
**Senior Software Developer** • Gary Teter
**Webstore Coordinator** • Rick Kunz

**Customer Service Team** • Sharaya Copas, Katina Davis,
   Sara Marie, and Diego Valdez
**Warehouse Team** • Laura Wilkes Carey, Will Chase,
   Mika Hawkins, Heather Payne, Jeff Strand, and
   Kevin Underwood
**Website Team** • Brian Bauman, Robert Brandenburg,
   Lissa Guillet, and Erik Keith

## DEAD SUNS ADVENTURE PATH

### PART 5 OF 6
# THE THIRTEENTH GATE

**THE THIRTEENTH GATE**                            2
by Stephen Radney-MacFarland

**RELICS OF THE KISHALEE**                         38
by Stephen Radney-MacFarland

**ALIEN WORLDS AND CULTURES**                      42
by Mikko Kallio, Jason Keeley, Lyz Liddell, Ron Lundeen, and Mark Moreland

**ALIEN ARCHIVES**                                 54
by Mikko Kallio, Jason Keeley, Lyz Liddell, Ron Lundeen, Mark Moreland, and
Stephen Radney-MacFarland

**CODEX OF WORLDS: URRAKAR**                       62
by Owen K.C. Stephens

**STARSHIP: MODIFIED ATECH BULWARK**        INSIDE COVERS
by Stephen Radney-MacFarland

This book refers to several other Starfinder products, yet these additional supplements are not required to make use of this book. Readers interested in references to Starfinder hardcovers can find the complete rules of these books available online for free at **paizo.com/sfrd**.

## ON THE COVER

Artist David Alvarez gives us a glimpse of Null-9, the crazed android in charge of the Devourer cult that edges closer to gaining control of a deadly ancient alien superweapon.

**paizo®**

Paizo Inc.
7120 185th Ave NE, Ste 120
Redmond, WA 98052-0577

**paizo.com**

# THE THIRTEENTH GATE

## PART 1: STATIC SUNS, CLOCKWORK PLANETS — 3

As the heroes near the alien megastructure known as the Gate of Twelve Suns, they must deal with a squad of Cult of the Devourer starships that want to see them dead.

## PART 2: COUNTDOWN TO OBLIVION — 10

The heroes must explore one of the gate's controller moons, fend off attacks from more Devourer cultists, and resolve a dispute between two ancient artificial intelligences while learning the awesome power of the Stellar Degenerator.

## PART 3: LAST GASPS — 27

The android leader of this sect of the Cult of the Devourer searches a second controller moon for a way to open the Gate of Twelve Suns. The heroes must put an end to her plans before the devotees of the Star-Eater gain control over a deadly superweapon!

## ADVANCEMENT TRACK

"The Thirteenth Gate" is designed for four characters.

**9** The PCs begin this adventure at 9th level.

**10** The PCs should reach 10th level before facing off against Malice.

**11** The PCs should be 11th level by the end of the adventure.

# ADVENTURE BACKGROUND

Millions of years ago, two advanced civilizations—the kishalee and the sivvs—clashed in an interstellar war that lasted for centuries. In a desperate bid to bring the conflict to a quick end, the sivv government funneled much of its wealth into the creation of a massive superweapon. Known as the Stellar Degenerator, the device was designed to vastly accelerate the rate of nuclear fusion in a star, quickly turning it into a cold, lightless, black dwarf star. Before the Stellar Degenerator could be tested, kishalee spies learned of its existence, providing enough intel for the kishalee military to launch a surprise attack on the sivvs and seize control of the weapon. Demoralized by the loss, and their economy in shambles with nothing to show for it, the sivvs were swiftly defeated and their territories annexed by the kishalee.

The kishalee took possession of the Stellar Degenerator, and though they fought many of other societies over the following centuries, they never felt endangered enough to use it... until they came into contact with a powerful and aggressive race that threatened to strike at the heart of kishalee civilization and destroy it utterly. After much deliberation, kishalee leaders authorized the use of the superweapon against the star of their enemy's home system.

As the system cooled and darkened, the dead sun's weakened gravitational pull was no longer able to hold the planets, which went flying off into space. While the resulting destruction and loss of life won the war for the kishalee, they were, as a society, horrified about what they had done. They concluded that the Stellar Degenerator should never be used again, but when many in the military raised the specter of another unwinnable war, the government decided to hide the superweapon instead of destroying it.

Using the immense amount of energy siphoned off during the Stellar Degenerator's one and only firing, the kishalee were able to create a pocket demiplane in which to store the superweapon and wrangle a dozen nearby stars to demarcate its location while maintaining its stability. Dubbed the Gate of Twelve Suns, this megastructure was a feat of magic and engineering that took decades to build. Once it was completed, kishalee military and scientific staff were placed in bases on each of the "controller moons" orbiting the twelve suns to monitor the demiplane and prevent anyone else from opening it. Though these personnel were swapped out regularly, the kishalee government foresaw the eventual need for automation should their civilization ever fall.

More decades passed as kishalee scientists worked to perfect a true artificial intelligence that could function indefinitely while managing the gravitational forces created by having a dozen stars in such proximity. They were unsuccessful until a pair of researchers named Eltreth and Osteth discovered a way to upload a consciousness into a mystically charged mainframe to create an immortal AI. However, they didn't want to ask anyone else to make such a sacrifice, so much to their colleagues' surprise, the two friends made a pact to go into this eternity together.

Their plan worked, and for uncountable ages, the two AIs dutifully defended the Gate of Twelve Suns against the ravages of entropy, even after the fall of their former civilization. But nothing in the universe can resist entropy's pull forever, and sometimes entropy fights back.

It started with digital whispers from the void, hovering on the edge of Eltreth's programming like a figment just barely perceived. Each time the AI hunted for the source of the discordance, he found nothing. Over a period of years and then decades, the voice persisted. It spoke to the nagging doubts in Eltreth's soul—fears that he was trapped within a virtual cage from which oblivion was the only escape. From there, it corrupted the AI's logic, making him believe that all beings were similarly trapped and that only he had the keys to their metaphysical jail: the Stellar Degenerator. By releasing the superweapon from its demiplane, the end of everything could begin; it would be a paean to the Devourer, the source of the voice polluting the AI's mind.

Eltreth's increasingly erratic behavior was not unnoticed by Osteth. She shunted his programming into a hardware prison, and there he stayed for over 2 centuries. Osteth continued her custodianship of the gate while searching for a method of purging Eltreth's corruption, but the Devourer's stain defied removal. Osteth had resigned herself to the possibility that her companion might have to be confined indefinitely, until the balance of power changed when a sect of the Cult of the Devourer called the Desperate Hunger arrived at the Gate of Twelve Suns. This dreaded band of murderous nihilists and their leader, a ruthless android named Null-9, were able to free Eltreth and place Osteth in his former jail, all in preparation to secure the Stellar Degenerator and achieve the Star-Eater's ultimate goal: the eradication of everything, everywhere.

# PART 1: STATIC SUNS, CLOCKWORK PLANETS

By the conclusion of "The Ruined Clouds," the PCs have learned about the existence and location of the Gate of Twelve Suns, the hiding place of the Stellar Degenerator, from the floating city of Istamak, a former kishalee colony. More importantly, they should have discovered they weren't the only ones to gain this intelligence: the Cult of the Devourer is one step ahead of the PCs. If the PCs have any chance

THE THIRTEENTH GATE

PART 1: STATIC SUNS, CLOCKWORK PLANETS

PART 2: COUNTDOWN TO OBLIVION

PART 3: LAST GASPS

RELICS OF THE KISHALEE

ALIEN WORLDS AND CULTURES

ALIEN ARCHIVES

CODEX OF WORLDS

of stopping the Devourer cultists from retrieving the Stellar Degenerator, they must speed from the Nejeor system to the gate's coordinates elsewhere in the Vast. This journey takes 5d6 days of Drift travel. If the PCs want to return to Absalom Station to resupply or purchase new equipment, this luckily adds only 1d6 additional days to the trip. The PCs aren't on a ticking clock, but if it seems like they want to dawdle, you should impress upon them that time is of the essence.

## EVENT 1: INEVITABLE CORRUPTION (CR 10)

The trip through the Drift to the Gate of Twelve Suns is not without peril. Strange storms of quantum foam and clusters of planar debris litter the nearby space during the journey, though these are easily avoidable and pose no threat to the PCs. However, when their starship approaches the end of the trip and passes through a nearly invisible cloud of dust, the vessel is boarded by a hostile intelligence!

**Creature:** Few creatures of the multiverse are more determined than inevitables, living machines forged in the planar city of Axis and imparted with unshakable purpose. Anhamuts are inevitables fashioned from millions of nanites and programmed to protect those who explore and chart the chaotic cosmos, though a few of them—known as Edgeseekers—move from planet to planet making their own surveys. The Edgeseeker named Quillius arrived at the Gate of Twelve Suns years ago by chance. Curious about the strange alignment of suns, Quillius has been examining the area for some time, and they were taken by surprise when a group of vessels—those belonging to the Desperate Hunger—appeared from the Drift a few days ago.

Edgeseeker Quillius approached and boarded the vessels in their discorporated nanite form to offer assistance to the travelers, not realizing the extent of the sect's evil. As the inevitable regained their solid form, the cultists attacked without a second thought, thinking Quillius some kind of avenging angel. Quillius made a fighting retreat back out into space, but before they could use their *interplanetary teleport* spell-like ability to reach safety, a terrible coincidence occurred: the inevitable was pulled into the Drift when someone somewhere fired up a Drift engine. The traumatic event fractured Quillius's mind, but in another phenomenal coincidence, the inevitable arrived very close to the PCs' starship.

The cloud of dust the PCs' starship passes through contains Quillius in their discorporated form. Their nanites are able to slip through microscopic cracks in the vessel's hull

and interface with the starship's computer. Quillius attempts to learn more about the PCs by hacking into their files. Quillius has a total bonus of +24 to their Computers checks. At this level, the base DC to hack the PCs' starship computer is most likely DC 29, unless the PCs have upgraded their systems. With a successful check, Quillius accesses the most basic information about the PCs' vessel. A PC who succeeds at a DC 28 Perception check or DC 22 Computers check notices that the ship's computers are being hacked into. If the PC's result exceeds the DC by 5 or more, the PC can tell that the hacking is coming from within the computer itself!

After 1 round, Quillius regains their solid form on the starship's bridge and pronounces a stuttering judgment against the PCs. Read or paraphrase the following.

---

"In-in-in-interlopers! You will cease your transgressions and r-r-r-return to your place of origin or be d-d-d-destroyed!"

---

A PC who succeeds at a DC 35 Mysticism check identifies Edgeseeker Quillius as an anhamut inevitable, an outsider tasked with protecting explorers of the galaxy. This fact alone should tip off the PCs that this creature is acting strangely—possibly from madness or another affliction—but if the PC's result exceeds the above DC by 5 or more or a PC succeeds at a DC 25 Sense Motive check, the characters realize this is certainly the case. However, this doesn't prevent Quillius from striking out at the PCs immediately after this speech.

The PCs can simply destroy the inevitable to stop the assault, or the heroes can attempt to parley with them in a number of ways. A successful casting of *charm monster* will calm Quillius down enough for the PCs to explain their position. If a PC casts *remove affliction* and successfully touches Quillius (by targeting their EAC with a melee attack) and succeeds at a DC 18 caster level check, the inevitable's mind is repaired and they will speak freely. In addition, a PC can attempt to change Quillius's attitude from hostile to unfriendly with a successful DC 44 Diplomacy check. It takes 5 rounds of combat to attempt this check, and worshipers of Triune gain a +1 circumstance bonus to this check. Once unfriendly, Quillius will stop attacking long enough to have a longer conversation. See Development for more results of such a conversation.

| QUILLIUS | CR 10 |
|---|---|

**XP 9,600**

Anhamut inevitable (*Starfinder Alien Archive* 66)

QUILLIUS

LN Medium outsider (inevitable, lawful)

**Init** +3; **Senses** darkvision 60 ft., low-light vision;
Perception +19

### DEFENSE                                              HP 180
**EAC** 23; **KAC** 24

**Fort** +11; **Ref** +9; **Will** +13

**Defensive Abilities** regeneration 5 (chaotic); **Immunities**
electricity; swarm immunities in discorporated form;
DR 10/chaotic; **SR** 21

### OFFENSE
**Speed** 30 ft., fly 40 ft. (Su, perfect, discorporated form only)

**Melee** nanite blade +21 (2d8+12 S; critical nanite burst
[DC 19])

**Ranged** electric discharge +19 (3d4+10 E)

**Spell-Like Abilities** (CL 10th)
1/day–*interplanetary teleport* (self plus 50 bulk
of objects)

### TACTICS
**During Combat** Quillius strikes out against whomever
attacked them last (and did the most damage), as long as
they can reach that target with their nanite blade, making
full attacks using their inevitable onslaught ability unless
they routinely miss due to the penalties. If prevented
from using their blade, Quillius uses their electric
discharge ability.

**Morale** Unless the PCs attempt to speak with Quillius (see
above), their assault is unrelenting. In their addled state,
they confuse the PCs for the Devourer cultists that
attacked them.

### STATISTICS
**Str** +2; **Dex** +3; **Con** +2; **Int** +5; **Wis** +2; **Cha** +8

**Skills** Computers +24, Culture +19, Diplomacy +24,
Engineering +24, Sense Motive +19

**Languages** truespeech

**Other Abilities** constructed, discorporation

**Treasure:** If the PCs agree to take Quillius's aid (see
Development below), the inevitable can impart a *nanite*
weapon fusion (*Starfinder Alien Archive* 67) to up to four
melee weapons. With a touch, part of the inevitable's nanites
surge onto each weapon. The armaments glow briefly for a
moment and then return to their normal appearance.

**Development:** Edgeseeker Quillius is not normally a
murderous creature, but their mind is broken. If the PCs can
get them to talk, they can refocus their thoughts and return
to a state of normalcy. Though they are unfamiliar with
the name "Gate of Twelve Suns," if provided a description,
they will admit to the PCs that they recently came across
the kishalee megastructure as part of their exploration of
the galaxy. They had only a short time to study the area,
and will impart to the PCs what they have discovered
(see The Gate System below). This information will help
the PCs navigate the area and prepare for the dangers that
lie ahead. In addition, Quillius makes the PCs aware of the

gravitational forces at play within the system that make it
difficult to navigate, and, if the PCs agree, the inevitable
programs a set of compensation equations into the heroes'
vessel's navigational computers (see Navigating the Gates
on page 10). Finally, they warn the PCs that these forces
make it impossible to successfully activate a Drift drive
within the system.

Quillius also mentions their altercation with a fearsome
group entering the system in an unsafe-looking fleet of
vessels. They note that they attempted to speak peacefully
with the group but were attacked for their trouble, and
though they escaped, they were summarily shunted into the
Drift by coincidence (or perhaps Triune's divine will). If asked,
the inevitable describes this hostile group as "very angry, but
somehow delighting in that anger. They wore spiked armor
decorated with a red-and-black circle." A PC who succeeds at
a DC 22 Culture check or DC 18 Mysticism check recognizes
this account as portraying cultists of the Devourer. From what
Quillius can remember, they encountered the cultists only a
few days ago.

If the PCs tell Quillius all that they know about the Cult
of the Devourer and the Gate of Twelve Suns, the inevitable
becomes quite serious. Read or paraphrase the following.

---

"This is very disturbing. If what you say about the Gate of
Twelve Suns and the Stellar Degenerator is indeed true, the
Cult of the Devourer must not succeed. The entire universe
is at stake! You must continue with haste to stop them.
While I am technically programmed not to interfere in the
discovery of this megastructure, such destructive power
cannot be loosed on the galaxy. I can offer you a modicum of
aid if you so desire. But you must not fail!"

---

After giving assistance to the PCs (see Treasure above),
Quillius asks to be returned to the Material Plane on the PCs'
vessel, after which they are able to teleport away.

**Story Award:** If the PCs manage to talk Quillius out of
fighting, grant them XP as if they had defeated the inevitable
in combat.

## THE GATE SYSTEM
When the PCs emerge from the Drift, they are still nearly a
day's travel from the Gate of Twelve Suns. As they approach,
it's obvious even from a cursory scan that the system is
not a natural phenomenon. A perfect circle of a dozen stars
appears stationary with respect to one another, maintaining a
perfect gravitational balance. This stability is maintained with
technomagical equipment thousands of years old, and it can
be redirected and focused to tear a hole in the fabric of the
universe–specifically, to open the gateway to the demiplane
that holds the Stellar Degenerator.

Using their vessel's scanners and succeeding at a
Computers check, the PCs can gain a few more details. The
amount of information they receive is determined by the

THE
THIRTEENTH
GATE

PART 1:
STATIC SUNS,
CLOCKWORK
PLANETS

PART 2:
COUNTDOWN
TO OBLIVION

PART 3:
LAST GASPS

RELICS OF THE
KISHALEE

ALIEN WORLDS
AND
CULTURES

ALIEN
ARCHIVES

CODEX OF
WORLDS

**GATE OF TWELVE SUNS**

CONTROLLER MOON

GATE 1

C

B

A

LANDING PAD

result of the check, as detailed below. Gaining Quillius's aid (see page 4) grants a +5 bonus to this check.

**15+:** Scans reveal that a single planet orbits each star at exactly the same distance. The planets have roughly the same diameter, mass, and rotational period. Even stranger, each planet's orbit is synchronized with all the other planets in the system so that every so often they all face the center of the circle of stars at the same time.

**20+:** The gravitational forces exerted by the twelve stars is in a delicate balance, achievable only with exacting measurements and more than a little magic. These forces make navigating through the system very difficult and using a Drift engine within the system impossible. The safest time to attempt to reach one of the planets is when its orbit reaches the point farthest from the center of the system, though it is by no means simple (see Navigating the Gates on page 10). In addition, eleven of the planets are lifeless hunks of rock with no atmosphere; only one can sustain life—it is, in fact, teeming with it. A single intact structure can be detected on that planet's surface.

**25+:** The occasional burst of gravitational energy emanates from each planet as it reaches the point in its orbit where it is closest to the center of the system. The energy comes from a hole in each planet's crust at the equator that seems to reach straight down to the planet's core. A PC who succeeds at a DC 20 Physical Science check deduces that the release of this energy likely keeps the system stable. A PC who

then succeeds at a DC 20 Mysticism check surmises that, if focused properly, the energy can be used to open a large portal to another plane.

**30+:** Deep scans of the system's planets reveal small cosmic strings—one-dimensional "defects" in the fabric of space that produce gravitational waves—mystically contained within each planet's core. These cosmic strings are maintained by massive technomagic devices kept in working condition by armies of maintenance bots.

Further information about the planet's internal mechanisms can be found on the kishalee computer systems in the control complexes located on any of the planets. See page 15 for details on how the PCs can access these systems.

## EVENT 2: BATTLE ON THE EDGE OF TWELVE SUNS (CR 10)

After the PCs complete their scan of the system, read or paraphrase the following.

---

From the vicinity of the nearest planet, a trio of ships approaches: one large ship and a pair of escorts speeding alongside. All sensors indicate that they are on an intercept course! The comm channels screech to life, and a gaunt man leers toward the camera lens. His skin is dark but is made nearly iridescent by a swirl of glowing nanites. Long, silver dreadlocks and an unkempt charcoal-colored beard frame his face. The distortion of the lens puts a shade of menace to the man's movements and appearance.

"Are you ready for the end?" The question hisses out from a mouth of brown crooked teeth; a yellowish, soapy spittle flies forth with every syllable uttered. "I am the agent of oblivion! I am the fang of the Devourer! I am the herald of annihilation. I will sing when your bodies—then only shells—drift and twirl through the void, charred amid the tangled wreckage of your ship, and your journey to nothingness is nearly complete!"

---

The speaker is the Jangly Man, second in charge of the Desperate Hunger sect (see page 11). For decades, he was a renowned pirate captain, but then he heard the call of the Devourer from the void, driving him mad. He joined with Null-9 and the two of them orchestrated a massive raid on an ATech shipyard several years ago, securing new vessels in the process. The Jangly Man serves as the captain of one of the larger starships—now named the *Singularity*—when Null-9 is busy with other matters.

The lurching and rambling madman goes on with his strange taunting and morbid celebration of the Devourer's will as his ships move to engage the PCs' vessel. He answers questions with biting and insane mockery as well as more exultation of the Star-Eater. His babbling rises to a frantic crescendo of hate and nihilism just before the starship combat begins.

Shadows flit behind the Jangly Man as he babbles verbosely, and a PC who succeeds at a DC 30 Perception or DC 25 Sense Motive check realizes his gibbering seems to contain coded orders to his crew of the *Singularity* and those flying the fighter escort. The code is tricky and hard to decipher, as the Jangly Man and his crew are practiced in its use. The PCs have 4 rounds' worth of communication with the Jangly Man before starship combat begins to attempt to interpret the cultists' code and negate the tactical advantages it gives them. During this time, each PC who can hear the Jangly Man speak can attempt a Sense Motive check to perform the discern secret message task, which is opposed by a single Bluff check the Jangly Man rolls each round; he has a total skill bonus of +21, and his coded rant ability means the PCs must roll twice on their Sense Motive checks and take the lower results. The PCs must succeed at three or more of these opposed checks to invalidate the cultists' advantage (see Starship Combat below), but a PC who fails the opposed check by 5 or more drastically misinterprets some aspect of the code, increasing the total number of successes needed by 1.

If the Jangly Man determines that the PCs have discovered he is using a code to give orders, he terminates the transmission with the PCs' ship.

**Starship Combat:** As the *Singularity* and its fighter escorts lunge toward the PCs' ship, a starship combat encounter begins. The rules for starship combat are detailed starting on page 316 of the *Starfinder Core Rulebook*. The *Singularity* is positioned 18 hexes away from the PCs' vessel, and the two ships should be facing one another. The Fang Fighters start adjacent to the *Singularity* at its port and starboard sides. If the PCs didn't succeed at breaking the Jangly Man's code, the Cult of the Devourer ships gain a +2 bonus to gunnery checks and Piloting checks for the first 2 rounds of the encounter. All enemy vessels fight until they have been reduced to 0 Hull Points.

In addition, when the science officer succeeds at a Computers check to perform the scan action against the *Singularity*, that PC notices the vessel is using an outdated and heavily modified communications array. This system is extremely prone to being hacked, and by doing so, the PCs have the opportunity to listen to communications coming into and leaving the *Singularity*. Hacking the system requires an additional successful scan action against the *Singularity* (which also reveals any information about the starship it would normally reveal). Maintaining this open channel requires no further actions.

Once the communications array is hacked, the science officer discovers the *Singularity* is in constant contact with the two Fang Fighters. These transmissions are not coded, and in them, the Jangly Man gives orders to his fighter escorts, as well as shares any information the *Singularity*'s science officer learns about the PCs' vessel. The first transmission includes the following statement.

---

"We must destroy them. The boss says none can be allowed to interfere with the plan."

---

As long as the PCs maintain the open channel, they gain a +1 bonus to gunnery checks when shooting at the Devourer ships and to the Piloting check to perform the evasive maneuvers stunt. Each round after the PCs hack the *Singularity*'s communications array, the *Singularity*'s science officer can attempt a DC 22 Computers check at the end of the helm phase (this doesn't take an action). A successful check means that the Devourer science officer realizes the communication array has been hacked and scrambles any further signals for the remainder of the starship combat.

## SINGULARITY — TIER 7
Modified ATech Bulwark (see inside front cover)
**HP** 170

## FANG FIGHTERS (2) — TIER 4
Tiny fighter
**Speed** 10; **Maneuverability** good (turn 1); **Drift** 2
**AC** 20; **TL** 20
**HP** 40; **DT** —; **CT** 8
**Shields** light 80 (forward 20, port 20, starboard 20, aft 20)
**Attack (Forward)** high explosive missile launcher (4d8), twin laser (5d8)

THE THIRTEENTH GATE

PART 1: STATIC SUNS, CLOCKWORK PLANETS

PART 2: COUNTDOWN TO OBLIVION

PART 3: LAST GASPS

RELICS OF THE KISHALEE

ALIEN WORLDS AND CULTURES

ALIEN ARCHIVES

CODEX OF WORLDS

**Attack (Aft)** coilgun (4d4)
**Attack (Turret)** high explosive missile launcher (4d8)
**Power Core** Pulse Green (150 PCU); **Drift Engine** Signal Booster;
  **Systems** basic mid-range sensors, mk 3 duonode computer,
  mk 4 armor, mk 4 defenses; **Expansion Bays** none
**Modifiers** +3 to any two checks per round, +2 Computers,
  +1 Piloting; **Complement** 2

## CREW
**Gunner** gunnery +7
**Pilot** Piloting +11 (4 ranks)

**Development:** If the PCs' starship is reduced to 0 Hull Points, the Jangly Man has the opportunity to board it and participate in the heroes' slaughter firsthand. Proceed to Shadowy Menace below, but the combat occurs on the PCs' starship instead of on the *Singularity*.

If the PCs reduce all of the Devourer starships to 0 Hull Points, they might think it wise to blow the Devourer cultists out of the sky. However, if the PCs hacked into the *Singularity*'s communications array, they hear a broadband transmission from the ship, regardless of whether the Devourer science officer scrambled the signal. If they didn't eavesdrop on the previous communications, the PCs can intercept this one with a successful DC 22 Computers check. The intended destination of the message is unclear, thanks to the system's gravitational anomalies.

---

"Our ship's been pushed through the Blood Door, boss. The interlopers are tougher than I thought—may the Devourer consume them! I'm sending out a long-distance transmission for more choirs to come, slit their throats, and feast on their remains!"

---

A PC who succeeds at a DC 20 Mysticism check knows that "pushed through the Blood Door" is a Devourer idiom for being killed. The PCs can't stop the transmission from their own vessel, but a PC who succeeds at a DC 18 Computers check realizes that if the PCs board the *Singularity* and gain control of its communications,

they can fake an "all clear" signal, which should hopefully prevent more cultists of the Devourer from arriving.

**Story Award:** If the PCs successful defeat the *Singularity* and its escorts in starship combat, award them 9,600 XP for the encounter.

## EVENT 3: SHADOWY MENACE (CR 11)
In order to stop the *Singularity*'s call for aid or to defend their own starship (depending on how they fared in the starship combat), the PCs will need to face off against the Jangly Man and a handful of oblivion shade spawn.

The PCs can easily pilot their vessel alongside an incapacitated *Singularity* and override its cargo bay airlock locks with a successful DC 20 Computers check. Use the interior map of the *Singularity* on the inside back cover to determine the best place for this encounter. Some suggestions are the destroyer's main corridor or within the galley or crew quarters.

Alternatively, if the battle takes place aboard the PCs' starship, you can use the map of the *Sunrise Maiden* on the inside back cover of *Starfinder Adventure Path #1: Incident at Absalom Station*, allowing the players to choose from where they wish to repel the boarders. Of course, if the PCs have upgraded their ship (or even acquired a different one), you might require a map of your own devising.

**Creatures:** By the time the PCs board the *Singularity*, the Jangly Man has slain his living crew as punishment for their failure in the starship battle. However, four oblivion shade spawn (created by the oblivion shade mystic Malice) lurk aboard the vessel, ready to repel any intruders. The oblivion spawn hide within the bulkheads of the ship and attempt to surround the PCs. They strike out just as the PCs come across the Jangly Man.

Alternatively, if the Jangly Man is boarding the PCs' starship, he brings along the four oblivion shade spawn to flit through the PCs' starship's hull and surprise the heroes as he makes his presence known.

**THE JANGLY MAN**

## THE JANGLY MAN                              CR 8
**XP 4,800**
Male human envoy
CE Medium humanoid (human)
**Init** +8;
**Perception** +16

## DEFENSE            HP 115 RP 4
**EAC** 20; **KAC** 21

**Fort** +7; **Ref** +9; **Will** +11

## OFFENSE
**Speed** 30 ft.

**Melee** tactical spear +15 (1d6+10 P)

**Ranged** liquidator disintegrator pistol +17 (1d10+8 A)

## TACTICS
**During Combat** The Jangly Man tries to keep his distance, supporting any allies with his clever attack and occasionally drawing fire onto himself.

**Morale** In truth a coward, the Jangly Man might attempt to bargain for his life using his treasure trove of credits (see Treasure below) as leverage, but he will only do so if it seems he has no other choice. He begs for a chance to flee the system, worried about Null-9 learning of his timidity.

## STATISTICS
**Str** +2; **Dex** +4; **Con** +1; **Int** +2; **Wis** +0; **Cha** +6

**Skills** Acrobatics +16, Athletics +16, Bluff +21, Intimidate +21, Sense Motive +21, Stealth +16

**Feats** Dive for Cover

**Languages** Common

**Other Abilities** coded rant, envoy improvisations (clever attack, improved get 'em)

**Gear** kasatha microcord III (*haste circuit* and infrared sensors), liquidator disintegrator pistol (*Starfinder Adventure Path #2: Temple of the Twelve* 52) with 2 batteries (20 charges each), tactical spear; **Augmentations** disquieting nanites (see the sidebar).

## SPECIAL ABILITIES
**Coded Rant (Ex)** The Jangly Man is an expert at passing secret messages through his ravings. Whenever a creature attempts a Sense Motive check to discern a secret message he is passing, that creature must roll twice and take the worse of the two results.

## OBLIVION SHADE SPAWN (4)      CR 5
**XP 1,600 each**

NE Medium undead (incorporeal)

**Init** +5; **Senses** blindsight (life) 60 ft., darkvision 60 ft.; Perception +16

## DEFENSE            HP 65 EACH
**EAC** 17; **KAC** 18

**Fort** +4; **Ref** +4; **Will** +10

**Defensive Abilities** incorporeal; **Immunities** undead immunities

## OFFENSE
**Speed** fly 40 ft. (Su, perfect)

**Melee** incorporeal touch +12 (1d4+4 A; critical corrode 1d4)

## TACTICS
**During Combat** Each oblivion shade spawn focuses on a different target, hoping to quickly drain the entire party.

**Morale** The oblivion shade spawn continue to fight until they are destroyed.

---

## DISQUIETING NANITES

The Jangly Man uses a cybernetic augmentation that was originally stolen during the Desperate Hunger's raid on a remote tech factory and that he modified to intimidate his foes.

### DISQUIETING NANITES (CYBERNETIC)

**SYSTEM** Skin and Throat

**PRICE** 10,000            **LEVEL** 8

This augmentation infuses your skin with a host of iridescent nanites that swirl in hypnotic patterns. Internally, some of the nanites cluster around your voice box, slightly modifying your voice to create a kind of rhythmic reverberation. As a standard action, you can activate the nanites. After the first round, you must use a swift action each round to maintain the effect. A creature that can see or hear you when the nanites are activated must succeed at a Will saving throw (DC = 14 + your key ability score modifier) or be shaken for as long it can see or hear you and you continue the effect. If the creature succeeds at the saving throw, it is immune to the effect of the nanites for 24 hours. You can choose for the nanites to not affect allies. If the creature can both see and hear you, it takes a −2 penalty to the saving throw. This is a mind-affecting, sense-dependent effect. You can use the augmentation for 8 rounds per day, though these rounds need not be consecutive.

## STATISTICS
**Str** −; **Dex** +5; **Con** −; **Int** +3; **Wis** +2; **Cha** +2

**Skills** Acrobatics +16, Intimidate +16, Stealth +16

**Languages** Common

**Other Abilities** unliving, void leap

## SPECIAL ABILITIES
**Void Leap (Su)** See page 58.

**Treasure:** If the PCs have defeated the Jangly Man and his oblivion shade spawn allies on board the *Singularity*, they basically have the run of the vessel. Within the captain's quarters, tucked partially under the bed, is a dented steel box that holds half a dozen credsticks loaded with 25,000 credits in total. The *Singularity*'s crew quarters contains a battered but functioning suit of spider harness powered armor and a total of five shock grenades III and eight screamer grenades II scattered throughout the former crew's possessions.

**Development:** If the PCs are trying to end the *Singularity*'s call for aid, they can quickly reach the vessel's bridge after the battle. With a successful DC 25 Computers check, a PC can essentially send an "all clear" signal that piggybacks

## THE THIRTEENTH GATE

PART 1:
STATIC SUNS,
CLOCKWORK
PLANETS

PART 2:
COUNTDOWN
TO OBLIVION

PART 3:
LAST GASPS

RELICS OF THE
KISHALEE

ALIEN WORLDS
AND
CULTURES

ALIEN
ARCHIVES

CODEX OF
WORLDS

onto the other transmission, ensuring that no other cultists of the Devourer receive the Gate of Twelve Suns' coordinates. Quickly exploring the *Singularity*, the PCs can easily see that the vessel's power core is essentially damaged beyond repair, rendering the starship useless (except for as scrap, effectively reduced to the Build Points the PCs receive the next time they upgrade their vessel). In addition, the PCs discover the following message from Null-9 in the ship's logs. The woman's voice on it is authoritarian with a hint of an electronic rattle.

---

"If we can get the last console online, the weapon will be within our grasp, and soon the end of all things will follow. Unfortunately, the control board is shot. Zaz has no idea how to repair it, but Eltreth has told us where to find spares. Take the *Singularity* and patrol the system in case that inevitable managed to send for help. Bring some of Malice's children. I will contact you again to return to the control center when we have the control board."

---

A PC who succeeds at a DC 20 Culture check can surmise the voice is most likely that of an android.

If the PCs defeat the Jangly Man on board their own ship, the remaining crew on the *Singularity* succumbs to cowardice and flees the system. Either way, the PCs can move into orbit around Gate 1 (see Navigating the Gates below) and continue to the rest of the adventure.

## PART 2: COUNTDOWN TO OBLIVION

Once the PCs have defeated the Jangly Man and his crew, they have gained nearly unfettered access to the system of the Gate of Twelve Suns, as long as they navigate the area's strange gravitational forces carefully.

## NAVIGATING THE GATES

As the *Singularity* approached from the vicinity of the nearest planetoid (and since that world is the only one showing major signs of life), the PCs will probably want to start their explorations there. From the site of the starship battle, it takes 1d2 hours to enter orbit around that planetoid, which is made difficult by the gravitational fluctuations throughout the system. At the end of each hour of flight, a PC must succeed at a DC 25 Piloting check or the PCs' starship takes 4d8 damage to its hull, ignoring shields. Quillius's equations grant a +4 bonus to this check. A vessel in orbit is safe from these energies.

The PCs can discover these equations in other ways. If the result of the PCs' Computers check to first scan the system (see page 6) was at least 20, a PC can attempt a

DC 20 Physical Science check after an hour of calculations. If successful, the PCs can program their ship's navigational computers to gain the above bonus.

When the PCs travel from the planetoid housing the control center to the one housing the core facility in Part 3 (and back again), they will have to attempt similar checks. If the PCs search the control center's computers (such as the ones in area **C8**) for information about these gravitational irregularities and succeed at a DC 20 Computers check, they can download similar equations onto their datapads (and eventually their ship's navigational computers) to gain the +4 bonus to the Piloting check.

## GATE 1

The sun referred to as Gate 1 by the kishalee (and noted as such on the map) is the focal point of the Gate of Twelve Suns. Not only does the sole habitable planet in the entire system orbit Gate 1, but the star is also home to the control center for the dimensional portal. This facility housed the rotating staff that kept the megastructure functioning for a few hundred years after it was built, and it was also where the kishalee scientists Eltreth and Osteth enacted their bold plan to digitize their consciousnesses into true artificial intelligences (see Adventure Background on page 3).

When constructing the Gate of Twelve Suns, the kishalee endeavored to make the unnamed planetoid orbiting Gate 1 a place that would be hospitable to life, giving it an atmosphere and seeding it with flora and fauna. While the PCs are in orbit around the planetoid, they can do further scans on the celestial body, revealing the following information if a PC succeeds at a DC 15 Computers check. The planetoid has an oxygen-rich atmosphere and dynamic weather patterns. It supports one large ocean and a few small continents, whose biomes range from temperate plains to steaming jungles to polar ice caps; signs of life can be found all across the world. All of this normalcy seems to be maintained by technomagical ley lines emanating from tall antennae that encircle most of the planetoid, as the world's strange interior and the huge bore that runs through the center would most likely render the surface unlivable.

The PCs' ship's scanners also reveal a number of ruins scattered across the planetoid's surface and a single intact structure on the equator. A PC who succeeds at a DC 20 Physical Science check can tell that these buildings are thousands of years old. The intact structure stands in the middle of a dense jungle; the only safe place to land a starship is on a landing pad—no more than a deteriorating slab of an ancient concrete-like material—in a clearing half a mile away. It takes 1d2 hours for the PCs to land their starship on this pad, and this flying does not subject their ship to the dangers of fluctuating gravity. See A Wild and Alien World on page 12 for more information about the surrounding jungle area.

## THE DESPERATE HUNGER

The Desperate Hunger is a powerful wall breaker choir (for more information about Devourer cult terminology, see pages 46–49 of *Starfinder Adventure Path #2: Temple of the Twelve*) of Devourer cultists who have been tasked with taking control of the Stellar Degenerator in order to hasten the eventual end of all things. The men and women of the Desperate Hunger are more akin to a tribe than a company of soldiers. Instead of practicing drills, they indulge in murderous and obscene rituals. Status among the group increases only when an individual's body count rises, and its current roster boasts some of the most depraved psychopaths in the known universe. From Deldreg the Butcher to Sisyrus Coldblood, there is not an ounce of pity or compassion in the lot.

The villains of the Desperate Hunger fear very little—as those striving for the inevitable true death of the multiverse do not scare easily—but they all fear their leader, the heartless android Null-9. They fear her cold and calculating mind, and the way her words seem to bite into one's soul. This fear has been twisted into a kind of fierce loyalty, even though Null-9 makes it clear that she considers those under her to be simply fangs biting and breaking at her command. The android sees herself as a true chosen of the Devourer and is certain she will have a large part to play in bringing about the universe's last gasp.

The Jangly Man (whom the PCs have met and dealt with by now) was Null-9's second-in-command. She entrusted him with many of the sect's more delicate matters, as the human was the most charismatic of the bunch. While he preferred to use tactics of confusion and intimidation against those he faced, he had the capacity to be charming toward those he was courting for initiation into the cult.

The oblivion shade mystic Malice, a driven and quiet force that lingers on the edges of the choir, supports the other members of the Desperate Hunger whether they like it or not. While the cultists don't exactly fear her, they give her a wide berth, as the undead mystic can kill with a touch, pulling from her victim one of her spawn—creatures similar to her who are unquestionably devoted to her. The cultists have seen members of their company face such a fate, and in the chilling aftermath could find very little of their former companion's personality evident. Most of the other cultists agree that this is probably a fate worse than death, and so they are quick to follow Malice's twisted commands even when they run contrary to Null-9's wishes (though this rarely happens).

The oddballs of the group are the twin ysoki mechanics (otherwise known as degenerators) brought into the choir by Null-9 when she discovered them among the wrecked starship hulls of Akiton almost a year ago. Though the new recruits are often the subject of harsh practical jokes and derision, Xix and Zaz can give as good as they get. The brother-and-sister tinkerers craft elaborate mechanical devices to prank those

THE THIRTEENTH GATE

PART 1: STATIC SUNS, CLOCKWORK PLANETS

PART 2: COUNTDOWN TO OBLIVION

PART 3: LAST GASPS

RELICS OF THE KISHALEE

ALIEN WORLDS AND CULTURES

ALIEN ARCHIVES

CODEX OF WORLDS

who have humiliated them, sometimes leading to broken bones and lost fingers. Thanks to their killings during recent raids, the two ysoki are slowly gaining respect among the other cultists.

The cultists of the Desperate Hunger were the ones who attacked Istamak to find the location of the Gate of Twelve Suns before the PCs arrived in that city in the adventure "The Ruined Clouds." They sped off from the Nejeor system, information in hand, on their quest to find the Stellar Degenerator. Upon arriving at the system, they landed on the planet orbiting Gate 1. With ruthless efficiency, Null-9's forces burned their way through the jungle to the control complex and breached its meager defenses. The android then set Xix and Zaz to the task of discovering the building's secrets. The ysoki pair soon came into contact with Eltreth, the imprisoned artificial intelligence. He proved to be a surprising ally, as it became obvious that the alien AI had received revelations from the Devourer. Truly, Null-9 and the Desperate Hunger thought, their mission was blessed by the Devourer.

Though Osteth, the sane artificial intelligence, put up a fight, the ruthless band of cultists freed their new friend Eltreth and helped him place Osteth in his old virtual prison. However, Osteth was able to perform a few acts of defiance before she was sequestered away: she granted many of the megastructure's maintenance robots a degree of autonomy (a plan she had actually been working on for centuries), and she overloaded the circuitry of the control center's main computer, preventing access to the demiplane containing the Stellar Degenerator. By the time the PCs approach the gate system, the Desperate Hunger cultists have almost completed repairing the computer. They lack only a replacement control board, a bit of ancient kishalee technology. Eltreth has informed Null-9 that such a board can be located on one of the other controller moons. The android has taken some of her crew in a shuttle to the planetoid orbiting Gate 2 to retrieve the backup board, leaving Malice in charge of the control complex and sending the Jangly Man out to patrol the area in the *Singularity*.

## A WILD AND ALIEN WORLD

When the control center was staffed with living kishalee, the planetoid orbiting Gate 1 was seeded with all manner of flora and fauna. This helped keep the world habitable and gave the kishalee scientists monitoring the megastructure a way to stave off boredom and homesickness during their tours. Some constructed homes and farms miles away from the control center, living bucolic lives away from their place of work, while others would take extended vacations to explore the farthest reaches of the planetoid. The weather patterns and wildlife were tightly controlled with a series of technomagical antennae that projected a series of beams of energy encircling the entire world. With the fall of kishalee civilization, the artificial intelligences in charge of the Gate

of Twelve Suns could not spare resources to maintain these systems, and while they are automated enough to keep the oxygen levels and temperatures at optimal levels, they could not regulate natural evolution. After thousands of years, the plants and animals have experienced unchecked growth and natural selection.

Much of the planet's flora is poisonous, and some are downright predatory. They hide among the denser sections of foliage to lie in wait for a passing meal and then lash out with thorny vines that carry a paralyzing toxin. In addition, the descendants of docile herd animals have evolved into terrifying monsters. Some rampage through their territory, toppling trees and crushing smaller beasts with their powerful hooves, while others skulk silently through the brush, perfectly camouflaged until they leap at their prey, teeth and claws flashing.

As the PCs breach the cloud cover and make their landing approach, they catch glimpses of the planetoid's surface. They spot a stampede of wild, horned quadrupeds kicking up dust across a grassy plain. They skirt the edge of a mountain range and watch as an avalanche swallows a copse of tall trees. They pass over the canopy of a jungle, spooking a flock of brightly colored, double-billed birds. As they approach the landing pad identified in their scans, they can see a crude trail burned in the brush leading in the direction of the control center.

Landing on the pad takes no unusual effort, and no resistance meets the PCs on the ground. As they step out of their vessel, the PCs can easily spot the very wide path through the jungle. A PC who succeeds at a DC 25 Perception check or DC 20 Knowledge (nature) or Survival check notices that the densest parts of the foliage were recently cleared with fire, explosives, and sharp instruments. Walking the half mile to the control center looks like it will be smooth sailing.

As the PCs move through the jungle (use the map on page 6), they can hear screams and howls in the distance from the local fauna. Occasionally, carnivorous plants make half-hearted attempts to grab at the PCs with a green tendril, but this danger is easily avoided. A PC who succeeds at a DC 20 Knowledge (nature) or Survival check while examining the nearby plants can tell that many of them are poisonous. After about 5 minutes of walking, the PCs step into a swampy clearing where a major threat presents itself: a large and vicious beast bounds out of the jungle.

## A. JUBSNUTH ATTACK (CR 9)

As the PCs make the trek toward the control center, read or paraphrase the following.

---

The nearby trees sway as something very large barrels its way out of the jungle. Branches snap and foliage is scattered about as a large, bulbous beast with two mouths, each one dripping with slimy green saliva, bursts into the clearing. The creature

THE THIRTEENTH GATE

PART 1: STATIC SUNS, CLOCKWORK PLANETS

PART 2: COUNTDOWN TO OBLIVION

PART 3: LAST GASPS

RELICS OF THE KISHALEE

ALIEN WORLDS AND CULTURES

ALIEN ARCHIVES

CODEX OF WORLDS

C. CONTROL CENTER

1 square = 5 feet

walks on a handful of small legs, and two massive clawed arms jut from its torso. Its thick tail flails violently about, and both its mouths each let loose deafening roars as it charges forth.

Several inches of rainfall have collected in this natural depression within the jungle, making the ground damp and squishy. Bits of broken pavement jut from the mud at odd angles, remnants of the service road that once connected the landing pad to the control center.

**Creature:** Jubsnuths are the descendants of docile herd animals raised by the kishalee as food stock. Centuries of unchecked evolution have altered these creatures into murderous beats. More about jubsnuths can be found on page 57. While jubsnuths are typically deeply territorial and vicious, this particular specimen has been driven to an utter frenzy by the loss of its young.

## JUBSNUTH — CR 9
**XP 6,400**

**HP** 145 (see page 57)

### TACTICS

**During Combat** Not a subtle combatant, the jubsnuth bites, swallows, and tramples until it is the only creature left alive.

**Morale** In this type of rage, the jubsnuth continues its attack until it is killed or somehow restrained.

## B. THE WATCHER WITHOUT EYES (CR 10)

Before the PCs reach the control center, they have a chance to realize that something is watching them from above.

**Creature:** The Desperate Hunger is close to realizing its goal of claiming the Stellar Degenerator, and this has caught the attention of an atrocite, a native outsider that serves the Devourer. It has used its *plane shift* and *interplanetary teleport* spell-like abilities to reach the Gate of Twelve Suns, drawn to the cultists like a bee is drawn to a bloom. It has yet to reveal itself to the cultists and sees the PCs as nuisances it can take care of before doing so. The atrocite lands quietly behind the PCs and announces its presence with a telepathic shout of "Die!"

This atrocite appears as an androgynous human with a shaved head covered in scars. It has only hollow holes where its eyes should be, and a pair of fanged mouths open on its palms. A grayish haze tinged with crackling red lightning floats above it.

## ATROCITE — CR 10
**XP 9,600**

*Starfinder Adventure Path #4: The Ruined Clouds* 56

CE Medium outsider (chaotic, evil, native)

**Init** +2; **Senses** blindsense (life) 30 ft., darkvision 60 ft.; **Perception** +19

### DEFENSE — HP 147
**EAC** 23; **KAC** 22

**Fort** +9; **Ref** +9; **Will** +15

**Immunities** poison, vacuum

## OFFENSE

**Speed** 40 ft., fly 40 ft. (Su, average)

**Melee** slam +17 (2d8+15 B)

**Ranged** void bolt +19 (3d4+10 force; critical severe wound [DC 19])

**Spell-Like Abilities** (CL 10th; melee +18, ranged +19)

    1/week–*interplanetary teleport* (self only), *plane shift*

    1/day–*cosmic eddy* (DC 22), *enervation*

    3/day–*arcing surge* (DC 21), *bestow curse* (DC 21),
      *displacement*, *synaptic pulse* (DC 21)

    At will–*mirror image*, *see invisibility*

**DESPERATE HUNGER CULTIST**

**Offensive Abilities** words of destruction

## TACTICS

**During Combat** The atrocite casts *cosmic eddy* centered on the PCs in the first round of combat to hinder their movement. It then uses its ability to fly to try to stay out of the PCs' reach, blasting them with void bolts. If a PC scores a critical hit against the atrocite, it flies into a fury and descends upon that PC, making full attacks with its slam attacks.

**Morale** Not believing it can be defeated, the atrocite fights until it is destroyed.

## STATISTICS

**Str** +5; **Dex** +2; **Con** +2; **Int** +0; **Wis** +3; **Cha** +8

**Skills** Intimidate +24, Mysticism +24, Sense Motive +19

**Languages** Abyssal, Common; telepathy (100 ft.)

**Other Abilities** no breath

## SPECIAL ABILITIES

**Words of Destruction (Su)** Once per day as a swift action, the many mouths of an atrocite can speak words of total devastation. For the next 3 rounds, any chaotic evil worshiper of the Devourer within 60 feet adds the wound critical hit effect to all its attacks (in addition to any existing critical hit effect); if an attack already has the wound critical hit effect, it gains the severe wound critical hit effect instead. If the atrocite takes damage at any point during this 3-round period, the effects of its words of destruction end immediately.

## C. CONTROL CENTER

Eventually, the path through the harsh jungle turns into the remains of a battered road leading to a large structure. As the PCs approach, they can easily see the front doors of the building have been blown inward by some explosive force. This building is the control center for the entire megastructure.

    The control center is a bunker-like building constructed of a kishalee alloy that resists deterioration and the scourge of the elements. Even so, the jungle plants festoon nearly every exterior surface, and the occasional curious jubsnuth and other alien creatures have gnawed on the building's corners. Most of the building is still functional, though the thuggish and destructive Desperate Hunger cultists did some damage as they commandeered the place. Unless otherwise stated, all of the locations within the complex have the following traits.

    **Doors:** The doors within the control center are unlocked unless otherwise noted. They are opened by applying pressure to a triangular central panel at the center of each door. When opened, a door slides to one side. A door then stays open for 1 minute before closing automatically. Jamming a door open or closed requires a successful DC 17 Engineering check, or this can be done via hacking (see Computers on page 15). The doors are constructed of a reinforced variety of plastic and are about 2 inches thick (hardness 8, HP 50, break DC 20).

**Lighting:** Ceiling lights illuminate most places within the control center. The light is tinted green and is rather low, though not so much that it is considered dim light.

**Computers:** The first time the PCs try to hack any of the computers in the building, they find the programming language strange and unintuitive. Unless the PC attempting to hack a computer speaks Kishaleen (the language of the kishalee), the DCs of Computers checks to hack the computers in the control center are increased by 10. Once a PC succeeds at three Computers checks to hack the kishalee computers, she has figured out the unusual and strict logic of kishalee programming and can ignore the increase to the DCs no matter what languages she knows.

If the PCs gain root access to the control center's computer system, they can alter the level of lighting in each room, remotely open and close doors, and access ancient information about former control center personnel. Incredibly important functions, such as control of the demiplane, are restricted to one of the two AIs. See area **C4** for more information about joining the struggle between the two AI personalities.

Use the map on page 13 for the following areas.

## C1. Shattered Entrance

More of the jungle has been scorched here, most likely the result of a large explosion that has blasted a hole through the wall of a one-story building. Sounds of cruel laughter can be heard from inside.

When the Desperate Hunger cultists reached the control center, they found the front doors locked. The sect's degenerators, Xix and Zaz, had trouble hacking into the doors' opening mechanism, so they resorted to explosives. The resulting blast was so powerful that the entrance to the place is now a charred mangle of metal and melted plastic.

## C2. Wrecked Lobby (CR 10)

The remains of a large double door lies broken on the floor, while a couple of bizarre-looking chairs or couches sit mangled against the north wall. Two short sets of steps lead up to a raised section of the room, from which a double door exits to the north. A smaller door stands in the southeast corner.

This room served as a lobby and security checkpoint when living kishalee still used this facility. Once the AIs Eltreth and Osteth took over, this area sat unused for thousands of years, and a thick layer of dust covers much of the floor, disturbed only by the Devourer cultists' passing.

**Creatures:** Three of the Desperate Hunger cultists captured a velsasha—a furry, three-legged beast the size of a small dog with a spherical head on a skinny neck—that

wandered curiously up to the hole in the control center. They are now in the process of teasing and torturing their captive on the far side of the room. They laugh and shout cruelly as they batter the creature, and they are so focused on their morbid entertainment they don't notice the PCs' approach until the PCs make a great deal of noise or when they step more than 10 feet into the room. At that point, the cultists leap into action, grabbing either grenades or disintegrator pistols and drawing their blades. The velsasha attempts to flee the building, but may just cower in the corner to avoid explosions.

### DESPERATE HUNGER CULTISTS (3) ○ CR 7
**XP 3,200 each**
Human soldier
CE Medium humanoid (human)
**Init** +6; **Perception** +14

**DEFENSE**              **HP** 105 EACH
**EAC** 19; **KAC** 21
**Fort** +9; **Ref** +7; **Will** +8

**OFFENSE**
**Speed** 35 ft.
**Melee** sintered longsword +17 (2d8+14 S) or
    weapon spikes +17 (2d4+15 S)
**Ranged** liquidator disintegrator pistol +14 (1d10+7 A) or
    incendiary grenade II +14 (explode [10 ft., 2d6 F plus 1d6
    burn, DC 15])
**Offensive Abilities** charge attack, fighting styles (blitz), gear
    boosts (powerful explosive)

**TACTICS**
**During Combat** One cultists throws a grenade in the first
    round while the others start with shots from their
    disintegrator pistols before they charge up and enter
    into melee.
**Morale** Sadistic zealots who yearn for the end, these
    deviants typically fight to the death.

**STATISTICS**
**Str** +5; **Dex** +2; **Con** +4; **Int** +0; **Wis** +2; **Cha** +1
**Skills** Acrobatics +14, Athletics +19, Intimidate +14,
    Survival +14
**Feats** Step Up
**Languages** Common
**Gear** golemforged plating III (grim trophies, weapon spikes
    [tactical knife] [*Starfinder Adventure Path #2: Temple of
    the Twelve* 53]), liquidator disintegrator pistol (*Starfinder
    Adventure Path #2: Temple of the Twelve* 52) with 2
    batteries (20 charges each), incendiary grenades II (2),
    sintered longsword

**Treasure:** Three ancient kishalee hoverbikes, once used by the ancients scientists to get from dwellings long since crumbled to ruins, lean against the wall in one corner of the room. Two of them are still operational, but the third was critically damaged by the explosion that allowed the

THE THIRTEENTH GATE

PART 1:
STATIC SUNS,
CLOCKWORK
PLANETS

PART 2:
COUNTDOWN
TO OBLIVION

PART 3:
LAST GASPS

RELICS OF THE
KISHALEE

ALIEN WORLDS
AND
CULTURES

ALIEN
ARCHIVES

CODEX OF
WORLDS

cultists access to the control center. Within the closet on the southeast side of the room is a stand with four space suits constructed for kishalee anatomy. A secret compartment behind the stand (Perception DC 25) holds three temporal disruption grenades and a minor disruption pistol. With the exception of the space suits (which function as normal space suits), all of these kishalee relics are detailed starting on page 38.

**Development:** The Desperate Hunger cultists quickly grow bored, and they often break things, blow things up, and scuffle with one another to pass the time. As such, the sounds of battle here do not rouse the cultists deeper inside the building.

If the PCs capture one of the cultists, they get very little information without the help of mind-reading magic. A PC who aggressively interrogates a cultist and succeeds at a DC 24 Intimidate check to bully is rewarded only with rambling discourses on the destruction they've wrought here and elsewhere. If asked about their leader, the cultist says, "Don't cross Null-9. She'll feed you to that shadow. She says it's a blessing, but I'm not sure. Those made into her image seem lost in a place between here and oblivion." A cultist gives the same information if under the effect of *charm person* or similar spell but will obstinately refuse to answer questions when under the effects of a *zone of truth* spell.

If the velsasha remained within the room, it is wounded and scared. A PC can calm down the creature with a successful DC 12 Survival check to handle an animal (or lure it back to the door if it fled). From there, the PCs can use healing magic on the animal or use the treat deadly wounds task of the Medicine skill. A healed velsasha scampers back into the jungle with a happy trill. At your discretion, a PC with a connection to the natural world (or who wants a weird pet) might find the velsasha following him back to his starship later in the adventure.

## C3. Long Corridor

This corridor is the spine of the control center, connecting the various chambers in the building. Except for a few smears of grease and tracks in the dust, it is relatively free from the predations of the Desperate Hunger cultists.

## C4. Computer Lab

This large chamber is lit only by the bluish glow of a single monitor across from the southern door. The other computer consoles that line the walls are dark. A circular platform of some unknown technology is affixed to the floor in the center of the room. The view outside a window in the western wall is completely obscured by thick jungle foliage.

**OSTETH**

When Osteth noticed Eltreth's programming was becoming corrupted, she used the computers in this room—the very chamber in which they were both transformed into artificial intelligences—to create a prison for his virtual consciousness. Unfortunately, she was unable to stop the Desperate Hunger cultists from releasing Eltreth back into the systems and forcing her into this electronic jail.

The PCs can use the functioning computer panel on the far side of the room to begin accessing the control center's systems, though doing so is a challenge. The kishalee programming is unintuitive to those not steeped in kishalee culture (see the information on the control center's computers on page 15). If the PCs are familiar with the systems or can speak Kishaleen (see page 8 of *Starfinder Adventure Path #4: The Ruined Clouds* for more on Kishaleen), the base DC to access this tier 4 computer is 29.

Before they can get any information from the computer, the PCs must first hack into the system to gain access. Doing so triggers an alarm countermeasure, which sounds a harsh klaxon throughout the structure. A PC who succeeds at a Computers check to disable the countermeasure within 1 round of the alarm sounding manages to silence it before the cultists think to investigate. Otherwise, the cultists from area **C6** come to investigate 1 minute later (destroying the door to the chamber with a grenade if the PCs have jammed it shut). In either case, Eltreth is definitely aware the PCs have begun snooping into the computer system and attempts to find a way to further aid the Devourer cultists (see area **C5**).

Once the PCs have gained access to this terminal, they can power up the lights and the other computers in this room, which also allows Osteth to speak with them. When that occurs, read or paraphrase the following.

The platform near the center of the room flickers to life as a luminescent holographic projection manifests above it. Within seconds the light coalesces into a tall, regal humanoid form that resembles the images of the ancient kishalee found on Istamak. The figure is dressed in garb that appears to be a mixture of military and scientific outfits that seems to disappear into the glow of the circular dais at the figure's feet.

The holographic figure stretches out an arm and starts speaking strange, spidery syllables with the rapidity of purpose, though her expression remains fixed and stoic. If the PCs speak Kishaleen (or even Vulgar Kishaleen), they recognize that the figure is greeting them, though with some urgency. Returning the greeting in the same language means that the remainder of the conversation can then continue in Osteth's native language. If the PCs show any signs of consternation that they can't understand her, Osteth quickly probes their minds (this manifests as a slight tingling behind the eyes) and scans any visible pieces of technology on their persons to determine their preferred language. After a moment, an audio filter kicks in, and Osteth continues in Common.

---

"He has gone mad. His programming had degenerated and he kept raving about something called the Star-Eater. I confined him due to these critical errors, but now he is out, and I am in here! He and those who helped him must be stopped." There is a brief pause. "From your attire, I assumed you weren't allied with those cruel marauders. Please tell me you aren't with them."

---

The figure is the artificial intelligence Osteth, appearing as she did in life. The PCs can speak with her (in either her language or their own) to learn more about what is currently happening on the planetoid. Unfortunately, her programming has been sequestered to this chamber, and she can't aid them outside of it until Eltreth has been "captured" once again. Below are some common questions the PCs might ask and her responses.

**Who are you?** "My name is Osteth. I was once one of the many kishalee scientists who monitored this entire system, protecting its secret. Long ago, I had a physical form, but in order to maintain these computers past our civilization's fall, another engineer and I created digital versions of our consciousnesses to serve as custodians for eternity."

**Who is the other custodian?** "His name is Eltreth. We have operated here for millennia, keeping this place functional and its terrible secret hidden, until a couple of centuries ago. Without warning, he began to display signs of instability and critical errors. He became convinced that he was the tool of some being called the Devourer. I believed it to be just some sort of manifestation of degradation in his core programming, and I sequestered him to these servers before he could cause any damage. I had hoped he could be repaired, but recent events have changed my mind."

**What is this terrible secret you mentioned?** "Millennia ago, my people were locked in a war with a race called the sivvs. After decades of fighting, the sivvs fashioned a device of cosmic destruction known as the Stellar Degenerator and sought to use it to bring the kishalee to extinction. We captured the weapon before it could be activated and won the war. We then studied our spoils, learning much from its

dreaded power. We fired the Stellar Degenerator once… in self-defense, mind you! But the result was an atrocity could barely live with. We created the Gate of Twelve Suns—the star system in which you find yourself—to house and protect the weapon so that none might use it ever again." The PCs likely know much of this information, but you can use Osteth to fill them in on any part of the Adventure Path's backstory they might need to know.

**What is going on now?** "Several days ago we were invaded by a group of raiders. Some of them looked much like yourselves, but others were like figments, strange dark apparitions with no true form. The raiders call themselves the Desperate Hunger and are led by an android woman named Null-9—I discovered this as they blasted their way into this facility spouting paeans to this Devourer and caught me off-guard. Before I knew it, they had freed Eltreth and forced me into his prison. Luckily, I was able to place some roadblocks in their path to slow them down, but they cannot be allowed to access the Stellar Degenerator."

**What did you do?** "The many maintenance robots that perform the physical tasks of this system have always been semiautonomous, but ever since I locked Eltreth away, I have been striving to uplift the robots to full sentience so that they might continue should something happen to me. When it looked as though Eltreth would be freed, I uploaded as much independent programming as I could to their processors. It will take Eltreth some time to regain full control over those robots. In addition, I generated a pulse of electricity throughout the terminals in the operations room, making sure the demiplane containing the Stellar Degenerator could not be easily accessed."

**How do we stop Eltreth and the Desperate Hunger?** "Truthfully, I fear the Desperate Hunger will be stopped by nothing short of death. Then, though it pains me to say so, I must trap Eltreth again and destroy his programming for good. What I thought was a mere degradation was but utter corruption borne from powers I do not understand. If you know of any other way, please tell me."

**How do we free you?** "You cannot do it from here. You must access the sequestering subprogram from the main operations room." At this point, Osteth brings up a map of control center and points out area **C8**. "This should initiate an exchange of my core programming and Eltreth's. Beware, though. Eltreth has probably installed countermeasures."

**What are on the other planets?** "They hold small edifices deep within for monitoring the gravitational pulses that emanate from each planetoid's core. When my people were still alive, some of the scientists constructed personal laboratories in these facilities, but I haven't had need for them, so they have remained dormant for millennia." Osteth pauses for a second. "It is possible the marauders might be able to find replacement parts for the terminals I damaged on one of those bases. Once I have full access to the gate's systems, I should know more."

THE THIRTEENTH GATE

PART 1:
STATIC SUNS,
CLOCKWORK
PLANETS

PART 2:
COUNTDOWN
TO OBLIVION

PART 3:
LAST GASPS

RELICS OF THE
KISHALEE

ALIEN WORLDS
AND
CULTURES

ALIEN
ARCHIVES

CODEX OF
WORLDS

Osteth can't offer much more help to the PCs until she is restored to full functionality. She remembers the rough complement of the cultists (more than a dozen main members, an unknown number of shadow creatures, an android, and a couple of ysoki), but she has no means of knowing their current locations. She speaks freely about her role as the system's custodian, though she is clearly frustrated by how easily she was trapped in the prison of her own making. She muses that she may have done her job too well and wonders if similar feelings have compounded Eltreth's corruption. If the PCs spend too long speaking with her, she urges them to continue deeper into the control center and stop the cultists of the Desperate Hunger.

Except for the minor amount of information Osteth tells them, the PCs can learn nothing more about the Gate of Twelve Suns and its operation from the terminals in this room. These interfaces are purposefully isolated from the other computers of the control center and so have very little functionality.

SISYRUS COLDBLOOD

However, a PC who succeeds at a Computers check to manipulate a secure data module can discover detailed reports about Eltreth and Osteth's experiments on creating artificial consciousness. Though the equipment still remaining in this chamber is insufficient to upload another soul into the mainframe, the information within grants the PCs a +4 circumstance bonus to Computers checks to defeat Eltreth's countermeasures when attempting to restore Osteth (see area **C8**).

## C5. Robot Command Terminals (CR 9)

This rectangular chamber has various illuminated panels and monitors along its walls. Some show what looks like the schematics of the entire structure, while others seem to show the interior of the planet. In the latter images, squads of robots skitter along the technology-studded walls of a massive tunnel. A circular platform stands in the center of the room, projecting a hologram of a tall figure clad in white robes. The figure gestures at the various screens, seemingly attempting to direct the robots in their tasks.

The hologram is the projection of Eltreth, the kishalee AI working with the Cult of the Devourer. The PCs have walked in on him trying to reprogram some of the maintenance robots working in the interior of the planet to leave their posts and aid the Desperate Hunger cultists, but it is a nearly impossible task. As a failsafe after confining Eltreth's consciousness, Osteth reinforced the semiautonomous programming of the robots. It would take the Devourer-corrupted AI weeks—if not months—to reestablish full control of these robots.

If the PCs explored area **C4** and triggered the alarm countermeasure, Eltreth is aware there are intruders and realizes there is a chance they have already spoken to Osteth. Even if the alarm wasn't triggered, he guesses that the PCs might be some force sent here to stop the Desperate Hunger cultist's plan and knows he must slow them down, if not stop them. In the efforts to gain information about these strangers so he can relay it to Malice in area **C8**, he greets the newcomers as friends and potential saviors. He says the following in Common (having already learned the language from the cultists).

"Oh, thank the First Cause! I thought I was going to be stuck with these lunatics forever. You are here to help, yes?"

Eltreth isn't very good at bluffing; he has a total bonus of +8 to his Bluff skill checks. A PC who succeeds at an opposed Sense Motive check realizes the hologram is lying, as his tone is too sickeningly sweet and insincere. Still, he continues to plead, trying to get as many PCs into this chamber before setting off a vicious physical countermeasure (see Trap below). When he does so, he disappears from this platform, escaping to the holographic dais in area **C8**.

**Trap:** The ceilings, floors, and walls here are lined with conduits that act similarly to a shock grid computer countermeasure. Eltreth, in his position as an AI, can trip this trap with a thought, filling the room with deadly arcs of electricity. This has the side effect of destroying this room's electronics. The PCs might not have a chance to notice or disable the trap before it is triggered unless they keep Eltreth talking long enough for a PC to get a look around the room and attempt to hack the countermeasure remotely.

## ELECTRIC CONDUITS TRAP                          CR 9
**XP 6,400**

**Type** technological; **Perception** DC 33; **Disable** Computers DC 28 (defeat countermeasure)

**Trigger** special (see above); **Reset** none

**Effect** arcs of electricity (8d12 E); **Reflex** DC 18 half; multiple targets (all targets in area **C5**)

**Treasure:** A long-forgotten but still functioning sovereign helm and three kishalee batteries are stashed in a hidden compartment among the panels of this chamber. The compartment (which is shielded from the arcs of electricity) can be spotted with a successful DC 25 Perception check (which is reduced to DC 20 if Eltreth was able to set off his trap). More about these kishalee relics can be found on pages 38–41.

**Development:** The computers in this room have only holographic interfaces, not physical ones, and can be accessed only by someone who can do so remotely and wirelessly. If the PCs are familiar with the systems or can speak Kishaleen, the base DC to use the Computers skill on these tier 4 computers is 29 (see the information on the control center's computers on page 15). Once the PCs have access, they can see that Eltreth was attempting to reestablish direct control over many of the gate's maintenance robots, and that Osteth's counterprogramming would take a long time to undo. However, if a PC succeeds at a second Computers check to manipulate a control module within the system, she can see that several robots have gone "off the grid" both here in the control center and on the planetoid orbiting Gate 2. That PC can surmise that another hacker must have discovered a back door in the programming, allowing a partial (and probably temporary) rewrite of their directives. The computers in this room don't connect to the gate's main controls or the sequestering subprogram mentioned by Osteth.

## C6. DUSTY QUARTERS (CR 11)

A single, oddly shaped desk is all that remains of the furniture in this room. Piles of dust have collected in the corners, and pieces of random detritus are scattered across the floor.

Millennia ago, when small shifts of kishalee kept watch over the control center, this chamber served as a barracks. Once Eltreth and Osteth took over, this room went unused, gathering dust for thousands of years.

**Creatures:** While Null-9 and her crew are on the controller moon orbiting Gate 2 looking for a new control board and Malice is learning more about the Gate of Twelve Suns' operation from Eltreth, a few rank-and-file cultists wait in these quarters. They are very bored and restless but while under the stern gaze of Sisyrus Coldblood have yet to devolve into tearing down the walls. The half-orc woman acts as Null-9's quartermaster and, with harsh words and the occasional corporal punishment, keeps the other cultists from mutinying.

If the alarm from area **C4** is activated, the cultists here spring into action. They gather their weapons and move to investigate area **C4** within 1 minute, with Sisyrus egging them on. Otherwise, the PCs find the cultists in an inattentive state, throwing pieces of sharp metal at the far wall. They scramble for their weapons when they notice the PCs, chuckling with sadistic glee at the chance to fight.

## DESPERATE HUNGER CULTISTS (3)                    CR 7
**XP 3,200 each**

**HP** 105 each (see page 15)

### TACTICS
**During Combat** The cultists, eager for battle, close to melee range, waving their swords.

**Morale** None of these fanatics fear their own demise. They fight to the death.

## SISYRUS COLDBLOOD                                CR 8
**XP 4,800**

Female half-orc operative

CE Medium humanoid (human, orc)

**Init** +9; **Senses** darkvision 60 ft.; **Perception** +22

### DEFENSE                                         HP 115
**EAC** 20; **KAC** 21

**Fort** +7; **Ref** +10; **Will** +11

**Defensive Abilities** evasion, orc ferocity, uncanny agility

### OFFENSE
**Speed** 40 ft., fly 30 ft. (jump jets, average)

**Melee** tactical knife +15 (2d8+12 S)

**Ranged** advanced shirren-eye rifle +17 (2d10+8 P) or red star plasma pistol +17 (1d8+8 E & F; critical burn 1d8)

**Offense Abilities** debilitating trick, trick attack +4d8, triple attack

### TACTICS
**During Combat** Sisyrus stays in the back attempting to pick off enemies with her sniper rifle but will enter melee combat when needed.

**Morale** Sisyrus has never backed down from a fight, and she sure isn't going to start now. She fights until her last breath.

THE THIRTEENTH GATE

PART 1: STATIC SUNS, CLOCKWORK PLANETS

PART 2: COUNTDOWN TO OBLIVION

PART 3: LAST GASPS

RELICS OF THE KISHALEE

ALIEN WORLDS AND CULTURES

ALIEN ARCHIVES

CODEX OF WORLDS

## STATISTICS

**Str** +4; **Dex** +5; **Con** +3; **Int** +1; **Wis** +2; **Cha** +2

**Skills** Acrobatics +17, Athletics +17, Culture +22, Intimidate +22, Stealth +22, Survival +22

**Languages** Common, Orc

**Gear** advanced lashunta tempweave (*haste circuit*, jump jets, targeting computer), advanced shirren-eye rifle with 8 sniper rounds, red star plasma pistol with 1 battery (20 charges), tactical knife, credstick (2,500 credits)

**Treasure:** Though the last living kishalee in the building cleared out most of the items in the room, a few items were accidentally left behind in the closets. A pair of dimensional comm units and two kishalee batteries lie on the table (see page 40). The cultists have not figured out their secrets and see them as interesting but useless junk.

**Development:** Any attempt to interrogate a captured cultist here has the same results as interrogating one in area **C2**.

XIX

## C7. Ancient Workshop (CR 10)

This area is a cluster of workstations, crates filled with cast-offs of kishalee technology, and piles of tools, most alien but a few similar to designs used by Pact Worlds engineers. A pair of unusual robots lie lifelessly on the main worktable near the center of the room. A double door leads out to the south.

When the control center was more active, this chamber served as a workshop for the repair of malfunctioning maintenance robots and other equipment. In the intervening millennia, Eltreth and Osteth would usually direct the robots to repair each other on the job, occasionally sending robots too broken to be efficiently fixed to this room to power down permanently. The semiautonomous programming Osteth installed in the robots has them continuing this particular cycle.

**Creatures:** When Zaz left with Null-9 to find a new control board, Malice ordered the ysoki's sister, Xix, to try to repair the control board. In truth, Malice just wanted Xix out of her sight. The void shadow finds the twitchy ysoki irritating, and Xix is frankly scared to death of the mystic, so such an exile was perfectly fine with the mechanic.

Since Xix has learned enough about kishalee technology to know that the control board is fried and beyond repair, she has instead spent her time fiddling with the alien technology in this room. In addition to her drone, Xix has a pair of modified maintenance bots protecting her. She is responsible for hacking into a few of the robots' programming, enabling them to be temporarily controlled by either her or her brother. He took most of them with him and Null-9 to the planetoid orbiting Gate 2 for both defense and to aid in searching for a working control board. Xix knows that this control will be overwritten by the robots' normal programming in a matter of days, and hopes that her brother returns with them before that, as she is a bit savvier with computers than him.

Of the two ysoki degenerators, Xix is the more chaotic, her mind flitting from idea to idea with the speed of a hummingbird. In the past, Zaz has always had to bring her back to reality when she lost focus on the task at hand. However, when the two joined the Desperate Hunger and became full devotees of the Devourer, a new purpose took root in Xix's brain. She can see how her every action contributes to the eventual deterioration of the universe, and she delights in each explosion and gunshot. Now surrounded by the remnants of a civilization long since extinct, Xix pursues chaos with additional fervor. Underneath it all, though, the ysoki is still afraid to die, meaning there is a chance to encourage her to surrender if the battle isn't going in her favor.

When the PCs enter the room, Xix immediately sets the robots and her drone on the PCs, talking all the while. She peppers them with questions about who they are and why they are here as much as she peppers them with gunfire. Though she seems interested in the PCs' responses, she generally responds with assurances that what they want doesn't matter, as everything they love will eventually die or turn to dust and the universe will be consumed by entropy. She says these terrible things in a casual, upbeat way, as if she were pleasantly discussing the local weather.

As noted in her stat block, when Xix is reduced to fewer than half her Hit Points, she becomes open to a cease-fire. While she doesn't propose such an option herself, a PC who succeeds at a DC 24 Sense Motive check notices that Xix is speaking less and grimly concentrating on the fight, as if she suddenly realized she might lose. At this point, a PC can perform the combat banter action and attempt a DC 28 Diplomacy check to suggest to Xix that she surrender. If the PC succeeds at the check and promises not to kill her, Xix capitulates. The PCs can attempt this check a second time on a failure, though the second proposal must include a reassurance of transport off the planet (or some other equally enticing offer), in addition to a promise of mercy for Xix before she will consider it. After a second failure, Xix becomes resolved to fight to the death. See Development on page 22 for ways Xix might be able to help the PCs if she surrenders.

## MODIFIED MAINTENANCE BOTS (2)                        CR 6
**XP 2,400 each**
N Small construct (technological)
**Init** +6; **Senses** darkvision 60 ft., low-light vision; **Perception** +13

### DEFENSE                                               HP 80 EACH
**EAC** 18; **KAC** 19
**Fort** +3; **Ref** +3; **Will** +7
**Defensive Abilities** nanite repair; **Immunities** construct immunities
**Weaknesses** vulnerable to critical hits, vulnerable to electricity

### OFFENSE
**Speed** 15 ft., climb 30 ft., fly 20 ft. (Ex, average)
**Melee** slam +15 (1d6+11 B)
**Ranged** focused-beam laser +13 (1d6+6 F)

### TACTICS
**During Combat** The maintenance bots attack all creatures other than Xix and her drone, using their mobility to get above and around the PCs.
**Morale** Unless they are called off by Xix, the robots fight until they are destroyed.

### STATISTICS
**Str** +5; **Dex** +2; **Con** —; **Int** +3; **Wis** +0; **Cha** +0
**Skills** Acrobatics +18, Athletics +13, Computers +18, Engineering +18
**Languages** Kishaleen

### A CAPTIVE XIX

The PCs might not think leaving Xix alone on their starship while they explore the core facility on Gate 2's controller moon is a good idea. If they do, feel free to have the ysoki tinker with their vessel's systems. How much this mucking about damages the starship is up to you; it could be as benign as altering the functions of the buttons in the lavatories or as serious as a critical damage effect that isn't discovered until the PCs engage in starship combat (or if a PC succeeds at a DC 28 Engineering check the next time she boards the vessel).

On the other hand, if Xix is with the PCs when they fight Zaz, the reunion could go poorly for the PCs. At first, it might seem as though Xix is unconcerned with her brother's welfare. However, if the PCs reduce Zaz to fewer than 25 Hit Points, Xix goes berserk, attacking the character who damaged Zaz the most with an unrelenting fury. In this instance, Xix fights to the death and the sight of his sister in battle causes Zaz to hold his ground in area **D7** (instead of fleeing to Null-9's side). Don't award the PCs XP for defeating Xix a second time if this happens.

### SPECIAL ABILITIES
**Nanite Repair (Ex)** A maintenance bot's nanites can heal it, restoring 6 Hit Points per hour. Once per day as a full action, a maintenance bot can restore 3d8 Hit Points to itself or any touched construct with the technological subtype.

## XIX                                                    CR 8
**XP 4,800**
Female ysoki mechanic
CE Small humanoid (ysoki)
**Init** +4; **Senses** darkvision 60 ft.; **Perception** +21

### DEFENSE                                                HP 115
**EAC** 20; **KAC** 21
**Fort** +9; **Ref** +9; **Will** +9
**Resistances** electricity 5, sonic 5

### OFFENSE
**Speed** 30 ft.
**Melee** tactical knife +15 (2d4+9 S)
**Ranged** advanced semi-auto pistol +17 (2d6 P)
**Offensive Abilities** overload (DC 18)

### TACTICS
**During Combat** Xix starts combat by attacking the intruders with her pistol, while directing her drone Q-0 to close with the PCs. She instructs Q-0 to make melee attacks against the PCs, spending the extra action required to have the

THE THIRTEENTH GATE

PART 1: STATIC SUNS, CLOCKWORK PLANETS

PART 2: COUNTDOWN TO OBLIVION

PART 3: LAST GASPS

RELICS OF THE KISHALEE

ALIEN WORLDS AND CULTURES

ALIEN ARCHIVES

CODEX OF WORLDS

drone perform full attacks when it seems like Q-0 is hitting the PCs with regularity.

- **Morale** If Xix is reduced to fewer than half her Hit Points, her mood turns grim (see page 21). If the PCs talk her into surrendering, she calls off Q-0 and the maintenance bots.

### STATISTICS

**Str** +1; **Dex** +4; **Con** +2; **Int** +6; **Wis** +1; **Cha** +1

**Skills** Acrobatics +16, Computers +21, Engineering +21, Physical Science +16, Sleight of Hand +21, Stealth +21, Survival +16

**Languages** Common, Ysoki

**Other Abilities** artificial intelligence (drone named Q-0), cheek pouches, expert rig (hacking kit), mechanic tricks (ghost intrusion and repair drone), miracle worker 1/day, moxie, remote hack (DC 18)

**Gear** estex suit III (mk 1 electrostatic field, sonic dampener), advanced semi-auto pistol with 24 small arm rounds, tactical knife, custom rig, hacking kit, credstick (2,500 credits)

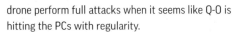

## Q-0                                        CR −

N Medium construct (technological)

**Senses** darkvision 60 ft., low-light vision; **Perception** +13

### DEFENSE                                        HP 90

**EAC** 18; **KAC** 20

**Fort** +6; **Ref** +6; **Will** +3

**DR** 1/−; **Immunities** construct immunities

### OFFENSE

**Speed** 30 ft.

**Melee** tactical swoop hammer +17 (1d10+11 B; critical knockdown)

### STATISTICS

**Str** +5; **Dex** +3; **Con** −; **Int** +2; **Wis** +0; **Cha** +0

**Skills** Athletics +18

**Languages** Common

**Other Abilities** reduced actions (*Starfinder Alien Archive* 138), unliving

**Treasure:** Two high-capacity kishalee batteries (see page 40) can be found in the triangular closet in the southwestern corner of the room.

**Development:** If Xix surrenders, she is actually open to answering questions. Some common queries and the ysoki's answers are below.

*Who are you?* "Name's Xix. They call me and my brother 'degenerators,' cuz we fix things. Well, fix 'em long enough that they can be used to break more things." She smiles widely and becomes momentarily lost in thought, remembering things she has smashed.

*Your brother?* "Zaz." She seems to be saying a name. "We used to live on Akiton before the pink-haired android found us and took us into space. He taught me everything I know about breaking things until I learned some stuff he don't know." She chews on her lip for a moment. "If you run into my brother, he probably won't be as interested in talking as I am. He's always been stubborn. You might have to kill him." This doesn't appear to upset her.

*Pink-haired android? Is that Null-9?* "Yeah, Null-9! Silly name. She's the one in charge of this whole operation. I don't know about her; she doesn't let me break all the stuff I want. Like, take this place. A dozen exploding suns would look so cool. But she says we gotta use 'em to get some kind of big weapon... from another dimension? Don't really know, don't really care."

*Where are your brother and Null-9 now?* "They took a shuttle off this planet to look for some kind of replacement part for one of the computers here. The glowing man told 'em should be able to find one inside one of the other moon's core facility or something. If they bring it back here, we can fix the computer, and then get that weapon Null-9's been talking about forever." The glowing man she is referring to is Eltreth, the kishalee AI.

*How many cultists are in this complex?* Xix asks who they've encountered by now, frowning at the mention of the half-orc Sisyrus Coldblood, calling her "no fun." She tells them who else is left in the control center, mentioning how many times she has tried to get the oblivion shade mystic Malice to teach her how to float through walls only to be stopped by her brother. She also lets the PCs know how many of the cultists left on the shuttle (which includes Null-9, Zaz, a dwarf named Deldreg the Butcher, six other cultists, three of Malice's spawn, and a handful of modified maintenance bots).

*Can you give us any help?* Xix laughs directly in their faces. "You're supposed to help me by not killing me!" A PC who succeeds at a DC 29 Diplomacy check can convince her otherwise. "The computers here are weird, but I noticed that the code uses a bunch of shortcuts that aren't really necessary, making it kind of easy to find loopholes." She teaches the PCs a couple of tricks to bypassing kishalee programming, granting them a +2 bonus to Computers skill checks to oust Eltreth. She otherwise refuses to fight her former comrades or do anything that will directly interfere with their mission.

Once the PCs are done asking Xix questions, they have to decide what to do with her. If allowed, she takes 10 minutes to repair Q-0 (if the drone was damaged), replenishing 10% of its total Hit Points. She agrees to stay put in this room while the PCs face Eltreth and Malice. The kishalee technology distracts Xix again the moment the PCs leave; she draws her pistol on them the next time they enter the room before she remembers who they are. If the PCs drag her along with them, she stands sullenly behind them during battles, mumbling to herself.

Unless the PCs specifically promised to help Xix off the planet, she doesn't realize that she will be stranded here when the PCs leave. However, when they return in Part 3, Osteth is adamant they take Xix somewhere else, as the ysoki has been threatening to dismantle many of the computer terminals within the control center. Bringing Xix with them to the controller moon orbiting Gate 2 might have negative consequences, as outlined in the sidebar on page 21. Xix's exact role in the next adventure (if she survives that long) is up to you.

**Story Award:** If the PCs get Xix to surrender, award them XP as if they had defeated her and the bots in combat.

## C8. CENTRAL OPERATIONS (CR 12 AND CR 10)

The northern door of this chamber opens onto a raised platform that overlooks various panels alight and abuzz with digital activity. Screens flicker with schematics of the many pieces of technology that control the kishalee megastructure, while others show views of legions of small robots repairing and maintaining massive mechanisms. The shadows here move strangely, seemingly having a life of their own. A circular dais occupies a second raised platform in the eastern end of the room.

This chamber holds the central control panels for the Gate of Twelve Suns. It was once staffed by a rotating contingent of kishalee technicians, though most of the systems were self-regulating. For millennia after, the AIs Eltreth and Osteth kept things running smoothly, usually only tweaking the gravitational output of one of the controller moons to keep the gate from tearing itself apart. In theory, the Gate of Twelve Suns could operate for eternity.

The lower half of this chamber holds the terminals that regulate the main functions of the megastructure, including the sequestering subroutine mentioned by Osteth. The upper section contains a holographic display dais similar to those in areas **C4** and **C5** and the controls that open the demiplane where the Stellar Degenerator is stored. If the PCs are familiar with the systems or can speak Kishaleen, the base DC to use the Computers skill on these tier 4 computers is 29 (see the information on the control center's computers on page 15). If the PCs have yet to meet Osteth, they can notice the existence of the sequestering subroutine with a successful DC 20 Computers check after they gain access. The PCs must succeed at three Computers checks to manipulate the module containing the sequestering subroutine in order to imprison Eltreth and free Osteth. However, the PCs will have to deal with the mystic Malice and her minions before they can even think about accessing these computers (see Creatures below and Traps on page 24).

**Creatures:** Malice, a number of her spawn, and a couple of Desperate Hunger cultists are holed up in the main part of this room after attempting and failing to take control of the Gate of Twelve Suns. Most likely, they will be aware of the PCs' insurgence into the building—warned either by the sounds of battle, the cultists in **C6**, or by Eltreth's encounter with the PCs. Even if the PCs can sneak up on the group, they will find them ready for a fight. Every creature in this room is willing to battle to the end in their desire to achieve the Devourer's ultimate goal. While the cultists are the first line of defense, the oblivion shade spawn quickly join them, while Malice stays back, using her spells and abilities to slow the PCs' approach.

### OBLIVION SHADE SPAWN (3) — CR 5
**XP 1,600 each**
HP 65 each (see page 9)

**TACTICS**

**During Combat** Unhindered by the terrain in this area, the oblivion shade spawn rush to flank the PCs to aid the cultists in defense of the chamber.

**Morale** Entirely the thralls of Malice's will, the oblivion shade spawn fight until destroyed.

### DESPERATE HUNGER CULTISTS (2) — CR 7
**XP 3,200 each**
HP 105 each (see page 15)

**TACTICS**

**During Combat** The cultists open with a volley of disintegration fire before engaging in melee combat. Their main goal is to stop the PCs from progressing farther into the chamber.

**Morale** These soldiers know what is at stake and will gladly sacrifice themselves for the cause. They give nor expect any quarter.

### MALICE — CR 9
**XP 6,400**
Female oblivion shade mystic (see page 58)
CE Medium undead (incorporeal)
**Init** +4; **Senses** blindsight (life) 60 ft., darkvision 60 ft.; **Perception** +22

**DEFENSES** — HP 120 RP 4
**EAC** 21; **KAC** 22
**Fort** +8; **Ref** +8; **Will** +14
**Defensive Abilities** incorporeal, share pain (DC 18); **Immunities** undead immunities

**OFFENSE**
**Speed** fly 40 ft. (Su, perfect)
**Melee** incorporeal touch +17 (3d4+9 A; critical corrode 1d6)
**Offensive** backlash (9 damage), create spawn, mental anguish (DC 18), sow doubt (4 rounds, DC 18)
**Mystic Spell-Like Abilities** (CL 9th)
    At will—*mindlink*
**Mystic Spells Known** (CL 5th; ranged +17)
    3rd (3/day)—*mind thrust* (DC 20), *ray of exhaustion* (DC 20)
    2nd (6/day)—*hold person* (DC 19), *hurl forcedisk*, *inflict pain* (DC 20), *mystic cure*
    1st (at will)—*detect thoughts*, *lesser confusion* (DC 18)
    **Connection** mindbreaker

**TACTICS**
**Before Combat** If warned of the PCs' approach, Malice

THE THIRTEENTH GATE

PART 1: STATIC SUNS, CLOCKWORK PLANETS

PART 2: COUNTDOWN TO OBLIVION

PART 3: LAST GASPS

RELICS OF THE KISHALEE

ALIEN WORLDS AND CULTURES

ALIEN ARCHIVES

CODEX OF WORLDS

readies an action to cast *ray of exhaustion* at the first PC through the door.

**During Combat** Malice begins combat by casting *mind thrust* and *ray of exhaustion* at the strongest-looking PCs. She continues to cast spells and use her mystic connection abilities to harry opponents until she is forced to engage the PCs in melee combat. If a cultist is wounded, she casts *mystic cure* on him to keep him in the fight.

**Morale** A true devotee to the cause of the Devourer, Malice continues her assault for as long as she exists. Even if she can't win the battle, she does all she can to weaken the enemies of the Star-Eater.

## STATISTICS

**Str** —; **Dex** +4; **Con** —; **Int** +3; **Wis** +6; **Cha** +2
**Skills** Bluff +17, Intimidate +17, Mysticism +22
**Languages** Common
**Other Abilities** unliving, void leap

**Traps:** Eltreth's image manifests on the holographic dais as the PCs battle Malice and her forces. He frets and reminds the cultists of their duty to the Devourer, but does nothing until the PCs attempt to access the terminals in the lower half of the room, which is most likely after the fight is over. Realizing that the PCs are likely to activate the sequestering program and put him back in his virtual prison, Eltreth becomes desperate. As the PCs attempt to use the Computers skill to hack the terminals and gain access, the AI establishes three countermeasures within the system that have the possibility of physically harming the PCs and making their task to free Osteth more difficult. Once the PCs have access to the computer system, a PC who succeeds at a DC 25 Computers check or DC 30 Perception check notices that some of the code is being rewritten on the fly from within—the result of Eltreth attempting to keep them from sequestering him.

If the PCs attempt to manipulate the module containing the sequestering subroutine without first disabling the first of the three countermeasures, Eltreth activates it, causing the terminal by the stairs that lead out of the room (marked with an X on the map on page 13) to explode in a shower of deadly sparks. Eltreth doesn't ready the second countermeasure trap until after the PCs succeed at the first Computers check to use the sequestering subroutine, so it can't be spotted or disabled until then. If the PCs attempt the second Computers check to use the subroutine before disabling the second trap, Eltreth activates that one, causing a terminal in the southeastern corner of the room (marked with an X on the map on page 13) to explode as well. The AI repeats this process one final time, destroying the console near the steps leading up to the holographic dais (marked with an X on the map on page 13). Since there are multiple terminals throughout the room, one PC can be attempting to activate the sequestering subroutine while another tries to find and disable the traps.

In addition to dealing electricity damage (see below), each countermeasure trap Eltreth successfully activates imposes a cumulative –2 penalty to Computers checks to manipulate modules or disable other countermeasure traps. Finally, if all three countermeasure traps are set off, the room goes dark and the sequestering subroutine can't be fully activated until a PC succeeds at a DC 30 Engineering check to repair much of the fried electronics (which takes 1d3 hours).

If the heroes manage to gain root access to these computer systems, they can stop Eltreth from activating any of the countermeasure traps.

## ELECTRIC COUNTERMEASURE TRAPS (3)    CR 7

**XP 3,200 each**

**Type** technological; **Perception** DC 30; **Disable** Computers DC 25 (disable countermeasure)

**Trigger** special (see above); **Reset** none

**Effect** shocking arc (4d12+4 E); Reflex DC 17 half; multiple targets (all targets within 20-ft. radius)

**Development:** Once Malice, her spawn, and the Desperate Hunger cultists are defeated and Eltreth has been imprisoned again, a sense of calm settles over the room. If the PCs have dealt with the other Devourer cultists in the facility, Osteth manifests her holographic form on the dais and beckons them to her. Continue with Osteth Restored below, as she informs the PCs that their work is not yet finished.

**Story Award:** If the PCs sequester Eltreth again and free Osteth, award them 6,400 XP.

## OSTETH RESTORED

When the entire control center has been secured, Osteth gives the PCs her gratitude. Read or paraphrase the following.

---

"Thank you, travelers. With Eltreth returned to his containment, the Gate of Twelve Suns is one step closer to being safe from the predations of those marauders. Now that I have access to the gate's full sensor suite, I can detect that some of them are still within the system. They are within the core facility of Gate 2's controller moon, an underground facility where my colleagues could adjust the gravitational pulses emanating from the planetoid's center when necessary. Since my inception as an artificial intelligence, physical presences have been unnecessary in those facilities, with the exception of standard maintenance bots, of course."

Osteth's form flickers for a moment. "It seems as though the marauders have briefly commandeered some of those robots to help them in their quest. I am completely locked out of those bots' programming, and it is only a matter of time before our enemies retrieve an intact control board required to repair the controls that open the Stellar Degenerator's demiplane. You must stop them!"

---

### WAITING THEM OUT

The players might wait for Null-9 to retrieve the control board and ambush her on her return. This means the PCs would have to fight Null-9, Zaz, Deldreg the Butcher, and all the rest simultaneously, which would be very difficult. Alternatively, the PCs might think to attack her shuttle as it leaves orbit from Gate 2's controller moon. In either case, you should prompt the PCs to be more proactive, using Osteth as your mouthpiece. If they are still reluctant to head to Gate 2's core facility, have Osteth contact the PCs with dire news: the marauders of the Desperate Hunger have discovered a way to open the demiplane from their current location. If the heroes don't rush to Gate 2 to stop them, the Devourer cultists will soon have access to the Stellar Degenerator! You can then run the encounters of area D largely as written.

---

Osteth answers any questions she can that the PCs ask about the Gate of Twelve Suns, the Stellar Degenerator, and the core facility on Gate 2's controller moon. She is able to provide them with a map of the core facility (see page 26) and informs them that, in addition to its standard function, the underground structure was occasionally used by kishalee scientists to examine the effects the megastructure's gravitational pulses had on living creatures, sometimes experimenting on test subjects transported from this controller moon's various biomes. In addition, Osteth informs the PCs that she registers nine organic life forms in the facility as well as a few anomalous energy signals that she finds confusing. If asked whether she believes they are more creatures like Malice the oblivion shade and her spawn, Osteth quietly agrees but doesn't sound very convinced.

Before the PCs leave for Gate 2, Osteth has one final thing to say to them.

---

"My new friends, with much time over the past few days in my confinement to think, I have come to a difficult conclusion. The Stellar Degenerator must be destroyed. Even if this Cult of the Devourer were defeated this day, there is no guarantee the location of the Gate of Twelve Suns will stay hidden. The sivv superweapon cannot be trusted with any people, no matter how peaceful and well intentioned they might be." She grows somber for a moment. "Though the events happened before I was born, I heard tales of when the kishalee used the Degenerator to 'pacify' a terrible enemy that threatened us with obliteration, and the results convinced my people to hide the weapon away."

Osteth's image disappears, and the entire room is filled with a holographic display of an unknown solar system. Her

## THE THIRTEENTH GATE

PART 1:
STATIC SUNS,
CLOCKWORK
PLANETS

PART 2:
COUNTDOWN
TO OBLIVION

PART 3:
LAST GASPS

RELICS OF THE
KISHALEE

ALIEN WORLDS
AND
CULTURES

ALIEN
ARCHIVES

CODEX OF
WORLDS

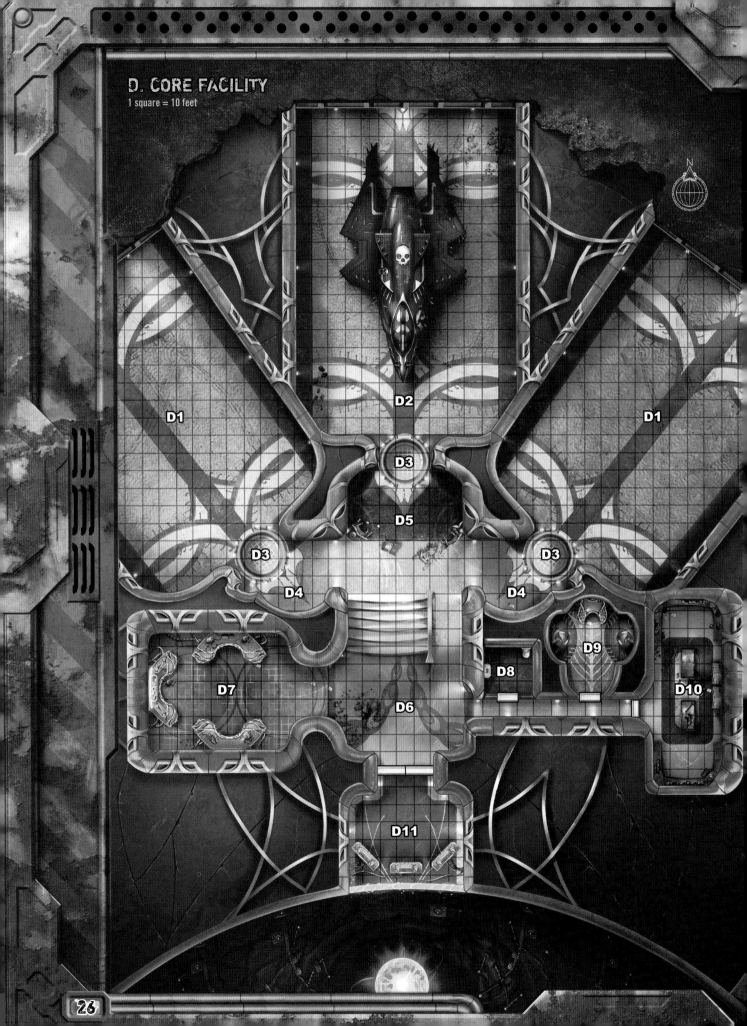

D. CORE FACILITY
1 square = 10 feet

D1

D2

D1

D3

D5

D3

D3

D4

D4

D9

D8

D7

D6

D10

D11

voice continues. "Some were killed instantly, caught in the energy transference beam when the Stellar Degenerator turned their sun into a black dwarf." The hologram shows a ray of light streaking in from outside of the system and hitting the sun. This tether pulses with energy, tearing apart starships and even moons in its general vicinity. "Those were the lucky ones. Within a week, temperatures across the system dropped to below freezing, and with no sun to sustain it, plant life began to die shortly thereafter." The sun at the center of system shrinks and grows dark. Digital displays appear near each of the system's ten planets, showing the decrease in temperature and light levels. "Hundreds of millions eventually starved to death or were killed in skirmishes over food." Another numerical display shows a rising death count. "The mass of the black dwarf wasn't enough to keep its planets in orbit, and eventually, they started to drift outward, spinning erratically into the inky depths." In the hologram, the orbits of the system's frozen planets wobble, and the farthest world disappears off the map. "A terrible way for a people to go extinct."

The lights in the chamber return to normal as Osteth reappears on her dais. "So you can see why the Stellar Degenerator must be destroyed. But to do so, we must first open the gate."

Osteth reiterates that the remainder of the Devourer cultists must be stopped, but she also says that the PCs should retrieve the control board those cultists are seeking. With the missing piece of equipment, Osteth can activate the Gate of Twelve Suns and release the Stellar Degenerator so that it can be destroyed once and for all.

## PART 3: LAST GASPS

The PCs' trip back to their starship is uneventful: the surrounding jungle seems to have gone quiet, as if the planet were holding its breath in anticipation. Entering orbit takes 1d2 hours, and traveling from the controller moon orbiting Gate 1 to the controller moon orbiting Gate 2 takes 1d8 hours. This is far less time than it would normally take to travel between two planets in the same system due to the constructed nature of the system and the gravitational anomalies that result from its strange composition.

Remember that at the end of each hour of travel between the gates, a PC must succeed at a DC 25 Piloting check or the PCs' starship takes 4d8 damage to its hull, ignoring shields. See Navigating the Gates on page 10 for more information about these checks. Once in orbit around Gate 2's controller moon, the PCs can scan that planetoid's surface.

## GATE 2

While Gate 1's controller moon was designed to support many forms of life, the other controller moons were left as stark and utilitarian hunks of rock with no atmospheres. Like the other controller moons, the one orbiting Gate 2 is essentially a container for a cosmic string that produces the gravitational waves that make navigating the system so tricky (but also keeps the system from tearing itself apart).

The PCs can make detailed scans of the planetoid as they orbit it, revealing the following information if a PC succeeds at a DC 15 Computers check. The planetoid has no atmosphere and shows no signs of life. There are no obvious kishalee-made buildings like those on Gate 1's controller moon, but there is a metal hatch—large enough for a Medium or smaller starship to fly through—in the planet's surface near the equator, similar to where the control center on Gate 1's controller moon was located. Further scans reveal an underground complex (with a breathable atmosphere and full gravity) located deep within the planet.

The hatch begins to open as soon as the PCs fly their vessel toward it, revealing a tunnel illuminated by strips of lights. It takes 1d2 hours to fly into the hatch and through the tunnel to a spot where it branches off into three sets of hangar bay doors. A red light glows above the center door, while green lights shine above the other two doors. As the PCs can bring their vessel near either the eastern or western set of doors, they open to reveal an empty hangar. The central doors remain closed if approached, the red light above flashing if the PCs' starship gets too close.

This middle hangar is occupied by the Desperate Hunger's shuttle, piloted here by Null-9 and the rest of her crew in their search to find a working control board. The safety precautions of the core facility don't allow the doors of an occupied hangar bay to open automatically, for obvious reasons.

If the PCs have a Large or larger starship, they will be unable to fly it into the tunnel leading to the hangar bays. However, they can land a Large starship on the planetoid's surface and move through the tunnel on foot. PCs with larger starships will have to think of their own way to get to the planetoid's surface. The controller moon has low gravity (except for within the core facility) and it takes 2d4+4 hours to reach the hangar bays (unless the PCs have a faster way of moving than their normal land speeds, such as a magical flight speed of 60 feet or more). The PCs can open either of the two empty hangar bays from the outside as described in area **D1**.

## OTHER GATES

It is conceivable that an unbroken control board can be found in any of the core facilities found on the other controller moons. Exploring these areas is beyond the scope of this adventure, but you can use the map of area **D** on page 26 as the map for the any of these facilities. The PCs will have to activate the facility's gravity, lighting, and oxygen for

THE
THIRTEENTH
GATE

PART 1:
STATIC SUNS,
CLOCKWORK
PLANETS

PART 2:
COUNTDOWN
TO OBLIVION

PART 3:
LAST GASPS

RELICS OF THE
KISHALEE

ALIEN WORLDS
AND
CULTURES

ALIEN
ARCHIVES

CODEX OF
WORLDS

**DISRUPTION GRENADE**

themselves, and they might have to fight off malfunctioning robots or unquiet dead at your discretion. If the PCs retrieve a control board from another facility, they will likely have to face off against the entirety of Null-9's remaining cultists in one large confrontation in the control center or during another starship combat and boarding encounter.

## D. CORE FACILITY

The core facility on Gate 2's controller moon is far under the planetoid's surface and allowed the kishalee custodians access to part of the bore that runs through the world. A pair of kishalee would travel to each core facility once a month to physically check over the computer systems. Of course, any emergencies would require additional visits. During the final years of the Gate of Twelve Suns being staffed by living beings, a few kishalee scientists used this core facility to conduct some of their own research, especially on how the system's gravity affects living things. Though the structure has no quarters for sleeping, these dedicated researchers would sometimes nap within the laboratory or a hangar bay.

The gravity, lighting, and oxygen were usually shut off in a core facility when not in use. Since the kishalee artificial intelligences were established millennia ago, no one had set foot in the core facilities until Null-9 and the Desperate Hunger arrived. The degenerator Zaz was able to get all of the systems online in short order and began working on establishing control of the local maintenance bots. When the PCs land their starship in one of the unoccupied hangars, Null-9 is very close to achieving her goal, with a few robots sent into the bore to retrieve a control board not being used by the technomagical machinery that keeps the cosmic string in the center of the planetoid contained.

By now, Null-9 has received the Jangly Man's final transmission and is aware that she could face the PCs at any moment. She has ordered a number of her cultists to defend the hallway between the core access (area **D11**) and her

shuttle, hoping that when she finally gets her hands on the control board, she can make a quick exit.

Unless stated otherwise, the areas of the Gate 2 core facility have the following traits.

**Computers:** The computers in the core facility run on the same programming as those found in the control center. By now, the PCs should have cracked the alien logic behind the kishalee coding (see page 15), but if they haven't (or don't understand Kishaleen), the DCs to hack any computers in this facility are increased by 10.

**Doors:** The doors within the control center are unlocked. They are opened by applying pressure to a triangular central panel at the center of the door. When opened, the doors slide to one side. They then stay open for 1 minute before closing automatically. Jamming the doors open or closed requires a successful DC 17 Engineering check, or this can be done via hacking (see Computers below). The doors are constructed of a reinforced variety of plastic and are about 2 inches thick (hardness 8, HP 50, break DC 20).

**Lighting:** Banks of harsh lighting attached to the ceiling illuminate most areas. The light here is white and brighter than that in Gate 1's control center.

If the PCs gain root access to the core facility's computer systems, they can alter the level of lighting in each room, remotely open and close doors, and access ancient information about the genetic experiments being performed here.

Use the map on page 26 for the following areas.

### D1. EMPTY HANGAR BAYS
The two areas marked **D1** on the map are functionally identical.

---

A few particles of dust swirl within this cavernous hangar bay. Its walls are made of a smooth, unknown metal without a trace of rivets or seams. A set of ship-sized doors stands opposite a smaller pair of convex doors.

---

While area **D2** currently houses the cultists' shuttle, both of these hangars are unused. The large hangar bay doors do not close until a starship makes a full landing on the floor. At that point, the bay repressurizes and fills with a breathable atmosphere, which takes approximately 15 minutes. The hangar bay doors open again only once the vessel inside takes off and internal sensors are sure no living creatures remain within the bay.

A smaller airlock built within the hangar bay doors can fit four Medium creatures or one Large creature. The airlock can be opened by anyone with the correct security clearance badge, but since those have been lost alongside kishalee civilization, a PC must succeed at a DC 28 Engineering check to access the airlock from either side. Once the PC is inside, the airlock can be cycled without a check.

When the PCs enter one of the two hangar bays (either in a starship or by foot), the facility's computers alert the Devourer cultists. They prepare for the PCs' arrival (see areas **D4** and **D5**).

## D2. Shuttle Hangar (CR 9)

The hanger bay where the Desperate Hunger's shuttle is docked is identical to the other two hangar bays. A small ramp leading into the vessel's interior was left lowered in case Null-9 and the rest of her crew want to leave in a hurry.

**Creatures:** A pair of oblivion shade spawn and two maintenance bots modified by the degenerators have been left here to guard over the ship. The two bots flank the ship's ramp, while the oblivion shade spawn stay hidden within the shuttle until a fight starts.

### OBLIVION SHADE SPAWN (2)                          CR 5
**XP 1,600 each**
**HP** 65 each (see page 58)

#### TACTICS
**During Combat** The oblivion shade spawn attempt to stay hidden within the hull of the shuttle until the bots commence with their attack, at which point they attempt to flank the PCs, focusing their attacks on spellcasters if possible.

**Morale** If at least one bot has been destroyed and the oblivion shade spawn have both been wounded, one of the spawn attempts to flee the hangar by flying down the lift shaft, warning any other cultists it finds on its way to Null-9 in area **D11**. The other spawn stays behind to stop the PCs from giving chase and fights to the death.

### MODIFIED MAINTENANCE BOTS (2)                    CR 6
**XP 2,400 each**
**HP** 80 each (see page 21)

#### TACTICS
**During Combat** The bots have been programmed to attack any creature that is not a member of the Desperate Hunger sect.

**Morale** With no contingencies for self-preservation, the bots fight until destroyed.

**Development:** If statistics for the shuttle are needed, use those for a Ringworks Wanderer (*Starfinder Core Rulebook* 310). However, Zaz has installed several security measures on the vessel to prevent anyone from flying off with it. Only Xix, Zaz, and Null-9 can access the ship's systems, thanks to a series of biometric locks. Due to several anti-hacking systems and some of the ysoki's own personal touches, the DC of the Computers check to bypass these locks is 35. In addition, anyone who fails a Computers check to bypass these locks activates a countermeasure that electrocutes her, dealing 8d6 electricity damage (Reflex DC 20 half). If activated, the countermeasure also fries part of the internal circuitry, imposing a –4 penalty on further Computers checks to hack into the systems; if the ship takes off in this state, its sensors start with the glitching critical damage condition. This critical damage condition can be repaired as normal (with 10 minutes of work and a successful DC 15 Engineering check).

## D3. Hover Lifts

Approaching the convex doors at one end of a hangar bay causes them to open automatically, revealing a 30-foot-diameter elevator car. Each of these hover lifts has simple controls on the inside: two blue lighted buttons aligned vertically. Pressing the lower button while on the hangar bay level causes the lift to glide downward about 200 feet; at the bottom of the shaft, the doors open to the corresponding area (either **D4** or **D5**). Pressing the upper button while on the hangar bay level causes the lift doors to open. While on the lower level, pressing the upper button sends the lift up to the hangar bay level and pressing the lower button opens the doors. It takes 90 seconds for the lift to ascend or descend from one level to the other.

After someone uses the lift, the car stays in its current position until a Small or larger creature approaches the doors on either level. If the PCs approach a doorway that is not at the lift's current level, the lift must climb or descend to that level before the doors will open, taking the usual amount of time to do so.

## D4. Welcoming Party (CR 9)

Although there are two areas marked **D4** on the map, the encounter with the Desperate Hunger cultists occurs only on the same side of the facility where the PCs have docked their starship. The two areas marked **D4** are identical mirrors of one another.

Smooth, gray walls and bright lighting accentuate the lack of corners in this entryway with a thirty-foot-high ceiling. The chamber opens onto a larger area just opposite a set of convex elevator doors.

This chamber, like all of those of the core facility level, was carved into the solid rock of the planet and reinforced with sheets of a nearly indestructible kishalee alloy. As the facility hasn't been occupied in millennia, the lack of atmosphere has helped preserve the paint on the walls and the integrity of the lighting. It gives the impression that the facility was built only a few decades ago instead of thousands of years. The only tip-off to the facility's age is the stale taste of the air.

**Creatures:** Two Desperate Hunger cultists stand their ground against the PCs as the oblivion shade spawn warns the rear guard in area **D5** of intruders.

### OBLIVION SHADE SPAWN                              CR 5
**XP 1,600**
**HP** 65 (see page 9)

#### TACTICS
**During Combat** The spawn slips away to warn the cultists in area **D5**, joining the fight there.

**Morale** If the spawn is reduced to fewer than 20 Hit Points during the battle in area **D5**, it attempts to flee to warn Null-9 in area **D11**.

THE THIRTEENTH GATE

PART 1:
STATIC SUNS,
CLOCKWORK
PLANETS

PART 2:
COUNTDOWN
TO OBLIVION

PART 3:
LAST GASPS

RELICS OF THE
KISHALEE

ALIEN WORLDS
AND
CULTURES

ALIEN
ARCHIVES

CODEX OF
WORLDS

## DESPERATE HUNGER CULTISTS (2)    CR 7

**XP 3,200 each**

**HP** 105 each (see page 15)

### TACTICS

**Before Combat** The cultists ready actions to shoot the PCs as soon as the elevator doors open.

**During Combat** The cultists attack the PCs with an unstoppable fervor.

**Morale** The cultists fight to the death.

## D5. REAR GUARD (CR 10)

The ceiling arches up to about fifty feet here, and at its apex hangs a glowing crystalline pyramid that sheds bright light on the room below. An array of upended tables and sturdy crates forms a makeshift barricade, blocking off much of the northern portion of the area, including a pair of shiny convex doors. Wide passages lead east and west, and a wide set of stairs leads down to the south. A declining ramp is separated from the stairs by a low metal partition.

This area has the same smooth, gray walls as those in areas **D4**, and the dramatic lighting fixture gives the impression that this is meant to be a grand entryway.

**Creatures:** Two berserkers (cultists of the Devourer who specialize in murder and mayhem, even more so than a standard member of the faithful) from the Desperate Hunger sect are stationed here to protect the entrance to the hangar bay containing their shuttle. They have looted kishalee grenades from the armory here and are eager to try them out. Unlike the cultists the PCs have encountered earlier, the berserkers' proximity to Deldreg the Butcher motivates them to a higher sense of discipline. They use the barricade for partial cover and remain in their relatively secure positions until the situation changes, even when the sounds of combat from area **D4** ring out.

## DESPERATE HUNGER BERSERKERS (2)    CR 8

**XP 4,800 each**

Human operative

CE Medium humanoid (human)

**Init** +8; **Perception** +17

### DEFENSE      HP 115 EACH

**EAC** 20; **KAC** 21

**Fort** +7; **Ref** +10; **Will** +11

**Defensive Abilities** evasion, uncanny agility

### OFFENSE

**Speed** 40 ft., climb 30 ft., swim 30 ft.

**Melee** tactical knife +17 (2d4+12 S)

**Ranged** liquidator disintegrator pistol +17 (1d10+8 A) or disruption grenade +17 (explode [20 ft., 2d10 So plus staggered, DC 18])

**Offensive Abilities** debilitating trick, trick attack +4d8, triple attack

### TACTICS

**During Combat** In the first round, the berserkers throw their newly found disruption grenades. While their barricade remains, they keep behind cover and attempt a trick attack every round with their pistols. Once the PCs breach the barrier, the berserkers start moving in and around the heroes, relying on the Mobility feat and the uncanny shooter operative exploit to avoid attacks of opportunity. They call over to Deldreg to be ready for a possible assault if the invaders seem to be winning.

**Morale** If one of the berserkers falls, the other attempts to make a break for area **D6** to support Deldreg's position.

### STATISTICS

**Str** +4; **Dex** +6; **Con** +2; **Int** +0; **Wis** +1; **Cha** +0

**Skills** Acrobatics +22, Athletics +22, Intimidate +22, Piloting +17, Stealth +17, Survival +17

**Feats** Mobility

**Languages** Common

**Other Abilities** operative exploits (uncanny shooter), specialization (daredevil)

**Gear** advanced lashunta tempweave (black force field [10 HP], disruption grenade (see page 39), liquidator disintegrator pistol (*Starfinder Adventure Path #2: Temple of the Twelve* 52) with 2 batteries (20 charges each), tactical knife

## D6. JUNCTION (CR 9)

This is a wide junction at the bottom of the stairs descending from the north. Hallways lead off to the east and west, while a large gray double door leads to the south. Sections of the floor have long gouges in them.

Shortly after arriving, the members of the Desperate Hunger used their weapons to damage the floor here out of boredom. When she saw this, Null-9 quickly gave them tasks to keep them occupied.

**Creature:** A berserker without equal, Deldreg the Butcher commands the awe and respect of many of the other cultists. Even outside of his ever-present suit of powered armor, the dwarf is as tough as nails and incredibly ruthless. He kills with a grim determination, drinks with gusto, and never backs down from a fight. However, he isn't stupid or tempestuous. He was given orders by Null-9 to hold this position, and does so even if he hears sounds of a fight in adjacent areas (especially area **D5**).

When the PCs first catch sight of Deldreg (likely when they are coming down the stairs), read or paraphrase the following.

Encased within a suit of battered powered armor, a scarred and gnarled dwarf stands in the center of the junction. He grinds his teeth on a frayed cigar, and bits of tobacco roll down his unkempt beard. An advanced X-gen gun is mounted on his shoulder, ready to unload a spray of death.

"You ready to dance?" The dwarf's voice grumbles, a hint of dark humor dripping from the question. "Ain't seen nothing but hunks of metal, weird plants, and people made of light since we came to this system, and I've been just aching for a dance."

No matter how the PCs answer him, Deldreg blasts away with his shoulder-mounted heavy weapon.

## DELDREG THE BUTCHER                              CR 9

**XP 6,400**
Male dwarf soldier
CE Medium humanoid (dwarf)
**Init** +9; **Senses** darkvision 60 ft.; **Perception** +17

### DEFENSE                                          HP 145
**EAC** 22; **KAC** 25
**Fort** +11; **Ref** +9; **Will** +10; + 2 vs. poison, spells, and
    spell-like abilities
**Defensive Abilities** slow but steady; **Resistances** cold 5

### OFFENSE
**Speed** 40 ft.
**Melee** unarmed strike +21 (2d8+20 B)
**Ranged** advanced X-gen gun +18 (2d12+9 P)
**Offensive Abilities** fighting styles (armor storm, blitz),
    traditional enemies

### TACTICS
**During Combat** The dwarf takes full advantage of his
    powered armor, typically clearing a path with automatic
    fire from his X-gen gun before entering into melee,
    throwing powerful punches at any target he can reach.
**Morale** If reduced to 40 or fewer Hit Points, he retreats
    to Null-9's side in area **D11** and aids her in escaping to
    the shuttle if needed.

### STATISTICS
**Str** +6; **Dex** +1; **Con** +4; **Int** +1; **Wis** +3; **Cha** –1
**Skills** Acrobatics +17, Athletics +22, Intimidate +17
**Languages** Common, Dwarven
**Other Abilities** stonecunning
**Gear** battle harness (mk 1 thermal capacitor),
    advanced X-gen gun with 100 heavy rounds,
    credstick (4,000 credits).

## D7. Robot Storage (CR 11)

This spacious chamber contains three tall racks holding various powered-down robots. Located in a central position, a freestanding control panel blinks serenely. A wide corridor leads out to the east.

The kishalee custodians would use the central control panel to activate replacement maintenance bots stored here. The maintenance bots rarely got damaged beyond repair, so these substitutes weren't used very often. This room saw

even less use when the artificial intelligences Osteth and Eltreth took control of the megastructure.

**Creatures:** When the ysoki degenerator Zaz saw this room, his eyes lit up. Null-9 has been unable to budge him from this spot since then, and she left a pair of cultists to watch over him while she continued the search for the control board.

Zaz has spent his time here attempting to activate the replacement robots in the hope that their programming won't contain the autonomy-granting subroutines Osteth put in place in the other robots. Though he and his sister (mostly his sister) have been successful in modifying a handful of these bots, Zaz wants to create a larger army in case the uncorrupted AI regains control. The ysoki knows his fiddling is ultimately unnecessary: when Null-9 retrieves the needed control board, they will return to Gate 1's control center to release the ultimate doomsday weapon and wreak havoc upon the galaxy. Until that time, though, Zaz is happy to tinker away.

When Zaz and the cultists hear the sounds of battle from area **D6**, they do not rush to aid the dwarf Deldreg.

DELDREG
THE BUTCHER

THE THIRTEENTH GATE

PART 1:
STATIC SUNS,
CLOCKWORK
PLANETS

PART 2:
COUNTDOWN
TO OBLIVION

PART 3:
LAST GASPS

RELICS OF THE
KISHALEE

ALIEN WORLDS
AND
CULTURES

ALIEN
ARCHIVES

CODEX OF
WORLDS

Zaz continues to tap away at the console, even though he has no chance of succeeding, and the cultists take up positions flanking the entryway, looking to ambush any PCs who enter the room.

## DESPERATE HUNGER CULTISTS (2) — CR 7

**XP 3,200 each**

**HP** 105 each (see page 15)

### TACTICS

**During Combat** The cultists engage the PCs in melee combat to protect their degenerator. Unless ordered otherwise, they stay by Zaz's side.

**Morale** The cultists fight to the death.

## ZAZ — CR 9

**XP 4,800**

Male ysoki mechanic

CE Small humanoid (ysoki)

**Init** +4; **Senses** darkvision 60 ft.; **Perception** +17

### DEFENSE                                            HP 135

**EAC** 22; **KAC** 23

**Fort** +10; **Ref** +10; **Will** +10

**Resistances** fire 5

### OFFENSE

**Speed** 30 ft., fly 30 ft. (jetpack, average)

ZAZ

**Melee** incapacitator +17 (3d4+11 B; critical staggered [DC 18])

**Ranged** minor disruption pistol +19 (2d6+9 So; critical staggered [DC 18])

**Offensive Abilities** overload (DC 18), target tracking, twin tracking

### TACTICS

**During Combat** While Zaz would prefer to avoid combat, he does not hesitate to fire his pistol at any creatures who threaten him. He avoids melee combat whenever possible.

**Morale** If reduced to fewer than 50 Hit Points, Zaz attempts to flee to Null-9 in area **D11**, ordering the cultists to cover his escape. If cornered or captured, he promises to take the PCs to his leader, but turns on the PCs as soon as he is in Null-9's company.

### STATISTICS

**Str** +2; **Dex** +4; **Con** +2; **Int** +6; **Wis** +1; **Cha** +3

**Skills** Acrobatics +17, Computers +17, Engineering +22, Intimidate +22, Sense Motive +17, Sleight of Hand +22, Stealth +22, Survival +17

**Languages** Common, Ysoki

**Other Abilities** artificial intelligence (exocortex), cheek pouches, expert rig (datapad), mechanic tricks (energy shield [15 HP, 9 minutes], resistant energy), miracle worker 1/day, moxie, remote hack (DC 18), wireless hack

**Gear** d-suit III (filtered rebreather, jetpack), minor disruption pistol with 2 kishalee batteries (see page 40; 20 charges each), incapacitator with 1 battery (20 charges), datapad, credstick (5,000 credits)

## D8. Unfortunate Prison (CR 12)

Although it has the same triangular touch pad as other doors, the door to this chamber doesn't open when the pad is touched. In fact, it blinks red instead. A PC who succeeds at a DC 25 Engineering check can remove the touch pad's cover and rewire it to get the door to open.

---

This circular chamber has stark white walls that are occasionally broken up by rectangular outlines near the floor and a few feet off the ground. The overhead lighting buzzes incessantly.

---

This chamber served as a single-person lavatory for the kishalee custodians who worked here, with the sink, toilet, and other sanitary devices emerging from the walls at a touch. The door can be opened from the outside only when the lavatory is unoccupied. The Desperate Hunger cultists didn't bother with this room when they couldn't immediately open the door.

**Creature:** When the living kishalee left the Gate of Twelve Suns, an unfortunate custodian named Abneth got locked inside the lavatory. His cries for help went unheard even by the artificial intelligences due to a blind spot in the facility's security apparatuses. Abneth died alone and terrified; soon after he rose as a marooned one, a particularly forlorn type of undead creature.

The undead Abneth slipped into a kind of torpor over the past millennia, still unable to free himself from his prison. If the PCs make any amount of noise at the lavatory door (such as by opening the touch pad), Abneth rouses from his slumber and begins banging on the door.

When the PCs open up the lavatory, Abneth lunges out and attacks the first living creature in his way. Abneth appears as a gaunt, desiccated kishalee wearing a clean set of white robes that have faded to gray with time.

## ABNETH                                          CR 12

**XP 25,600**
Male kishalee marooned one (*Starfinder Alien Archive* 76)
NE Medium undead
**Init** +5; **Senses** blindsight (life) 60 ft., darkvision 60 ft.;
    **Perception** +27

### DEFENSE                                        HP 185
**EAC** 26; **KAC** 27
**Fort** +17; **Ref** +11; **Will** +17
**Immunities** undead immunities

### OFFENSE
**Speed** 30 ft.
**Melee** ultrathin dagger +23 (4d4+20 S)
**Offensive Abilities** strangle (DC 21, 2d12+20 B, 1d4
    Con damage)

### TACTICS
**During Combat** Abneth is a straightforward combatant.
    He attempts to strangle those he can successfully
    grapple, falling back on his dagger if he can't pull off the
    combat maneuver.
**Morale** After being locked up for thousands of years, the
    only thing Abneth desires is to kill until he is destroyed
    or freed.

### STATISTICS
**Str** +8; **Dex** +5; **Con** —; **Int** +4; **Wis** +0; **Cha** +0
**Skills** Computers +27, Engineering +27, Life Science +22,
    Medicine +22, Physical Science +27, Stealth +27
**Languages** Kishaleen
**Other Abilities** sabotage life support, unliving
**Gear** kishalee holoarmor II (functions as squad hardlight
    series), ultrathin dagger

## D9. STRANGE MENAGERIE (CR 12)

Looking in on this room from the hallway, the PCs can see that it is dark except for a small red light blinking on a standby control panel on the far wall. As soon as a PC crosses the threshold of the doorway, a motion sensor in the ceiling activates the lights.

---

Two clear surfaces covered in alien writing hang on the walls near the only door leading out of this chamber. A computer terminal stands on the opposite end of the room. The main features of the room are two opaque cylindrical fields of energy near the walls, each about ten feet in diameter.

---

When the Gate of Twelve Suns was staffed with living beings, a handful of kishalee custodians took on their own projects during their tours in the megastructure. Laboratories like this one exist on many of the controller moons; this one was dedicated to examining the effects of the system's gravitational anomalies on other creatures.

A PC who examines the terminal and succeeds at a DC 20 Computers check determines that the cylinders of energy are acting as stasis fields for two living creatures. If the result exceeds the DC by 5 or more, the PC can also detect that the creatures are Large monstrous humanoids with bladelike arms. A PC who can understand Kishaleen can read the writing on the glass-like surfaces near the exit; they are filled with notes and formulae. A PC who succeeds at a DC 25 Life Science or Physical Science check can tell that the writing references both gravitational equations and biological processes. The notes are unfinished, though.

**Creatures:** The scientists' last experiments were on a pair of creatures transported from the mountainous regions of Gate 1's controller moon. Known as psitheers, these insectile humanoids have a hive-mind intelligence that aid them as they stalk their prey. Their arms end in vicious bladelike appendages that can cause terrible bleeding. The kishalee scientists wished to know the effects of high gravity on their exoskeletons but never completed their work, and, unthinking, left the two creatures in permanent stasis when they abandoned the system. Since the energy fields draw very little power, Osteth and Eltreth saw no need to shut them down.

During the Desperate Hunger's sweep of the facility, Zaz couldn't resist tampering with the stasis fields. He quickly reprogrammed the terminal so that the next person to access it causes the stasis fields to immediately shut down.

Once released, the psitheers attack all creatures in the room, confused and disoriented as to where they are and still in pain from the kishalee experiments performed on them long ago.

## PSITHEERS (2)                                   CR 10

**XP 9,600 each**
Variant Swarm thresher lord (*Starfinder Alien Archive* 110)
CE Large monstrous humanoid
**Init** +5; **Senses** darkvision 60 ft., blindsense (vibration)
    30 ft.; **Perception** +19

### DEFENSE                                        HP 165 EACH
**EAC** 23; **KAC** 25
**Fort** +14; **Ref** +14; **Will** +11
**Defensive Abilities** hive-mind intelligence; **Immunities** acid,
    fear effects

### OFFENSE
**Speed** 30 ft., climb 20 ft., fly 20 ft. (Ex, average)
**Melee** arm blade +23 (2d10+18 S; critical bleed 1d8)
**Space** 10 ft.; **Reach** 10 ft.
**Offensive Abilities** blade storm

THE THIRTEENTH GATE

PART 1: STATIC SUNS, CLOCKWORK PLANETS

PART 2: COUNTDOWN TO OBLIVION

PART 3: LAST GASPS

RELICS OF THE KISHALEE

ALIEN WORLDS AND CULTURES

ALIEN ARCHIVES

CODEX OF WORLDS

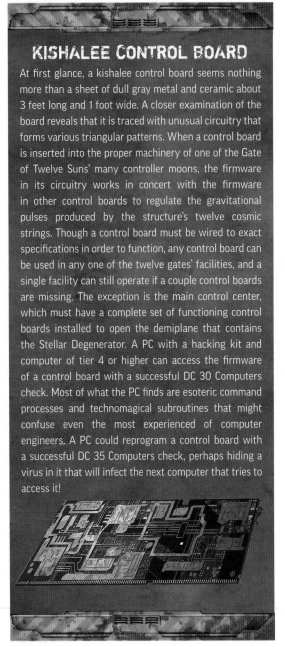

## KISHALEE CONTROL BOARD

At first glance, a kishalee control board seems nothing more than a sheet of dull gray metal and ceramic about 3 feet long and 1 foot wide. A closer examination of the board reveals that it is traced with unusual circuitry that forms various triangular patterns. When a control board is inserted into the proper machinery of one of the Gate of Twelve Suns' many controller moons, the firmware in its circuitry works in concert with the firmware in other control boards to regulate the gravitational pulses produced by the structure's twelve cosmic strings. Though a control board must be wired to exact specifications in order to function, any control board can be used in any one of the twelve gates' facilities, and a single facility can still operate if a couple control boards are missing. The exception is the main control center, which must have a complete set of functioning control boards installed to open the demiplane that contains the Stellar Degenerator. A PC with a hacking kit and computer of tier 4 or higher can access the firmware of a control board with a successful DC 30 Computers check. Most of what the PC finds are esoteric command processes and technomagical subroutines that might confuse even the most experienced of computer engineers. A PC could reprogram a control board with a successful DC 35 Computers check, perhaps hiding a virus in it that will infect the next computer that tries to access it!

### TACTICS
**During Combat** A psitheer slashes at the PCs nearest to it, using its blade storm ability to make three attacks as a full attack action whenever it can. It continues to fight in this way even if the attacks don't land with any regularity.

**Morale** The crazed creatures fight until they are destroyed.

### STATISTICS
**Str** +8; **Dex** +5; **Con** +3; **Int** −5; **Wis** +1; **Cha** −3

**Skills** Acrobatics +19, Athletics +19 (+27 to climb), Stealth +24

**Languages** none

### SPECIAL ABILITIES
**Hive-Mind Intelligence (Ex)** Psitheers are bound

together into a singular hive mind by a blend of exuded pheromones, imperceptible movements of antennae and limbs, electrostatic fields, and telepathic communication. All psitheers within 30 feet of each other are in constant communication; if one is aware of a threat, all are. (Such awareness can spread along a "chain" of psitheers under appropriate circumstances, potentially alerting distant psitheers.) In addition, once per round when within 30 feet of another psitheer, a psitheer can roll twice and take the better result on a saving throw against a mind-affecting effect.

**Treasure:** Within a hidden compartment beneath the computer terminal (Perception DC 28) there is a minor disruption rifle (see page 39) and a high-capacity kishalee battery (see page 40).

## D10. Ancient Armory

The eastern and western walls of this long room are lined with empty weapon racks, while the outlines of suits of armor can been seen inside of broken display cases along the northern and southern walls. The drawers of the two workbenches in the center of the chamber have been pulled out and their contents—empty cans of oil, tiny screws, and other bits of rusty metal—are scattered across the floor. A small compartment in the eastern wall hangs open, and a door exits to the west.

Despite the fact that the kishalee weren't at war with anyone when they built the Gate of Twelve Suns, they still kept the facilities stocked with armor and weapons just in case the megastructure was ever invaded by hostile forces. The kishalee custodians cleared out most of the armaments stored in this armory and weapons workshop when they left. The Desperate Hunger cultists plundered this room when they discovered it, finding a few weapons forgotten by the kishalee.

**Treasure:** Though the cultists discovered one of the room's hidden compartments, there are five others spaced around the room. Each compartment can be discovered with a successful DC 32 Perception check. The first compartment contains five high-capacity kishalee batteries. The second holds a cluster of three temporal disruption grenades. The third contains five disruption grenades, the fourth contains a minor disruption pistol, and the fifth contains a major disruption pistol. These items are described on pages 38–41.

## D11. Core Access (CR 12+)

This room buzzes with activity. Three control panels stand at the far end of the room opposite a double door to the north. The panels flash with multicolored lights and occasionally beep. The southern wall contains a large window, with some kind of shimmering containment field in place of glass. The vast bore that pierces the heart of the planetoid can be seen through the window. The walls of that massive cylinder are veined with strange conduits and studded with peculiar technology; countless maintenance robots, many so far away as to seem like mere insects, crawl over the various sections of the machinery, occasionally lit by a random spark of electricity. Monitors line the walls inside the room, showing close-ups of the robots working within the bore. One video stream tracks the progress of four such constructs, one of which is carrying a grayish rectangular object; these robots seem to be flying at all possible speed toward some point.

The gate's kishalee custodians used this area to monitor the progress of the continual maintenance of the machinery that holds this planetoid's cosmic string in place. A view of any of the hundreds of maintenance robots can quickly be brought up on one of the monitors with a few keystrokes. The containment field in the southern window keeps the oxygen from rushing into the vacuum of the planetoid's bore, but the maintenance bots (and other creatures) can easily pass through it.

**Creatures:** The android Null-9 paces between the control panels and the containment field. Though her eyes are cold and her movements regimented, she is almost trembling with anticipation. When the PCs enter the room, she addresses them with a flat voice that has a hint of metallic rattling.

"You are too late, meddlers. The end is nigh. I will prevail. I am the chosen of the Devourer, and you are just insects— insignificantly scrambling about ignorant of utter certainty."

With that, she lowers her weapon and fires.

Depending on how the encounters in other areas of the facility played out, Null-9 might be accompanied by Zaz, Deldreg, or both. Those two aid their leader as best they can, with Zaz taking cover behind one of the control panels and Deldreg rushing forward to punch PCs with his armored fist.

It takes 3 rounds from the start of combat for the four maintenance bots to reach this room, appearing just outside the containment field. On the fourth round on its initiative count, the maintenance bot with the control board moves to Null-9 and hands her the item. Once the android has the control board, her tactics change.

## MODIFIED MAINTENANCE BOTS (4)          CR 6
**XP 2,400 each**
**HP** 80 each (see page 21)

### TACTICS
**During Combat** After handing the retrieved control board to Null-9, the bots begin firing their lasers at the PCs, attempting to clear a path for Null-9.
**Morale** The bots fight until they are destroyed.

## NULL-9          CR 10
**XP 9,600**
Female android envoy/soldier
CE Medium humanoid (android)
**Init** +12; **Senses** darkvision 60 ft., low-light vision;
    **Perception** +19

### DEFENSE          HP 165
**EAC** 23; **KAC** 26
**Fort** +12; **Ref** +10; **Will** +11; + 2 vs. disease, mind-affecting
    effects, poison, and sleep

### OFFENSE
**Speed** 20 ft., fly 30 ft. (jetpack, average)
**Melee** weapon spikes +19 (2d4+15 S)
**Ranged** minor disruption rifle +22 (3d8+10 So; critical
        staggered [DC 17]) or
    temporal disruption grenade +22 (explode [20 ft., stunned
        1 round, DC 17])
**Offensive Abilities** fighting styles (sharpshoot), focus fire,
    sniper's aim

### TACTICS
**Before Combat** Null-9 activates her armor's force field.
**During Combat** Null-9 takes cover near the containment field
    and exchanges fire with the PCs until the maintenance
    robots show up with the control board. She avoids melee
    combat if she can, preferring to leave that to any allies in
    the room. Once the bots show up, Null-9 orders them to
    engage the PCs and throws a temporal disruption grenade
    at the heroes, hoping to slow them down as she makes
    her escape.
**Morale** If Null-9 gains the control board, is reduced to 40 or
    fewer Hit Points, or thinks her mission is in danger, she
    makes a strategic retreat to the shuttle. If it doesn't seem
    possible to make her way through the facility, Null-9 leaps
    through the containment field and uses her jetpack to fly
    to the planetoid's surface, but if she is surrounded, the
    android fights to the death.

### STATISTICS
**Str** +5; **Dex** +2; **Con** +2; **Int** +1; **Wis** +3; **Cha** +8
**Skills** Acrobatics +19, Intimidate +24, Piloting +19,
    Sense Motive +19
**Feats** Quick Draw
**Languages** Akitonian, Common
**Other Abilities** constructed, envoy improvisations (not in the
    face [DC 17], quick dispiriting taunt), flat affect, upgrade
    slot (jetpack)
**Gear** specialist defiance series (weapon spikes [tactical
    knife; *Starfinder Adventure Path #2: Temple of the
    Twelve* 53], white force field [15 HP]), minor disruption
    rifle with kishalee battery (20 charges; see page 40),
    temporal disruption grenades (3; see page 39), credstick
    (10,000 credits)

**Development:** If Null-9 makes her escape, this encounter could become a running firefight through the corridors of the

THE
THIRTEENTH
GATE

PART 1:
STATIC SUNS,
CLOCKWORK
PLANETS

PART 2:
COUNTDOWN
TO OBLIVION

PART 3:
LAST GASPS

RELICS OF THE
KISHALEE

ALIEN WORLDS
AND
CULTURES

ALIEN
ARCHIVES

CODEX OF
WORLDS

core facility (or perhaps up through the bore and onto the planetoid's surface).

If the android makes it back to her shuttle, she rushes inside and begins priming its thrusters, which takes 1 minute. If Zaz is with her, she orders him to sabotage the lift, hopefully buying them enough time to be able to take off and head back to Gate 1's control center. A PC can fix the elevator with a successful DC 30 Engineering check that takes 1 minute to attempt.

It takes an additional 3 rounds for the hangar bay doors to completely open, but only if there are no living creatures inside of the hangar bay (and not in the shuttle). Zaz can override this safety protocol, but if Null-9 is alone, she turns the shuttle's laser cannon on the doors; she must shoot them three times over the course of 3 rounds to blast them fully open. When either process starts, the atmosphere starts to rush out of the hangar bay. Any creature still in the hangar bay must succeed at a DC 35 Acrobatics or Athletics check saving throw each round or get pulled 10d10 feet toward the opening doors. If a living creature is forced out of the hangar bay doors, it immediately takes 3d6 bludgeoning damage (no saving throw) as it is buffeted against the walls and doors while being sucked out; unless it has protections against being in a vacuum, it then begins to suffocate and takes 1d6 bludgeoning damage each successive round (no saving throw). Unprotected living creature still in the hangar bay when the doors are completely open are also subject to this suffocation (but not the damage from buffeting).

If Null-9 escapes from the core facility, she flies her way back to Gate 1's control center. This could lead to another starship combat; use the statistics for a Ringworks Wanderer (*Starfinder Core Rulebook* 310) for the shuttle. Though the PCs' vessel likely outclasses the Desperate Hunger's shuttle, Null-9's goal is to reach Gate 1's controller moon, not to destroy the PCs. That doesn't mean she won't take a couple of potshots at the PCs if given the chance. She is much bolder in her flying if she has at least one ally still with her.

After all this, there is a slim chance Null-9 reaches the gate's control center. She is surprised to learn that Osteth has supplanted Eltreth and begins destroying computer terminals with unbridled ferocity. If the PCs confront her at this point, she blames them for her failure and fights to the death.

## OPENING THE GATE

Hopefully, the PCs have stopped Null-9 in one way or another and retrieved a working control board for Osteth. If the one control board is somehow broken or destroyed during the fight with Null-9, the PCs can have the maintenance bots fetch a new one from the core mechanisms of Gate 2's controller moon. This takes about an hour.

Returning to Gate 1's controller moon takes 1d8 hours. Since the system's gravitational forces are constantly in flux, at the end of each hour, a PC must still succeed at a DC 25 Piloting check or the PCs' starship takes 4d8 damage to its hull, ignoring shields. See Navigating the Gates on page 10 for more information about these checks. However, landing (which takes 1d2 additional hours but is not subject to the dangers of the fluctuating gravity) and traveling back to the control complex is uneventful.

Osteth is pleased to see the PCs again and inquires as to whether or not they were able to stop the Devourer cultists and bring back an unbroken control board. By inserting the control board into a slot she indicates under one of the central operation's terminals in area **C8**, the PCs have repaired the computers that can open the way to the Stellar Degenerator. Osteth repeats her insistence that destroying the superweapon is necessary, but she doesn't initiate the process to access its demiplane until the PCs are ready and the controller moons reach the innermost points of their orbits (which happens once a day). The characters can take as long as they want to rest up, heal, repair their starship, craft items, or even explore the other gates' controller moons as they see fit, though the kishalee AI starts to grow impatient after a few days.

If the PCs talk to Osteth about how they might be able to destroy the Stellar Degenerator, the AI admits that it will take an act of devastating power. The Stellar Degenerator was built as a weapon of war, after all, and can withstand a lot of punishment. It will likely take more firepower than the PCs' starship can bring to bear. Osteth has an idea that the Stellar Degenerator could be piloted into one of the gate's twelve suns, but someone would need to board the superweapon (which likely has ancient security measures still in place) and she is unsure how such an event would affect the rest of the system. She is fairly certain though that it will probably end in the death of whoever is at the Stellar Degenerator's helm. Osteth is open to hear the PCs' thoughts on the matter, but regardless of what the PCs come up with, any plan starts with accessing the demiplane in which the weapon is stored.

When the PCs give her permission to do so, a look of concern crosses Osteth's face. Read or paraphrase the following.

---

"My friends, something is terribly wrong. Thanks to the gate's advanced age, several microprocessors across the controller moons' core facilities are failing. Unfortunately, I have already initiated the subroutine to open the demiplane. My calculations predict that unless something is done in the next few minutes, a catastrophic chain reaction will destabilize the system's twelve cosmic strings and cause each and every one of the suns to be pulled into the center of the system. Such a collision would result in a massive supernova... and the Stellar Degenerator would remain safe within its demiplane!" The consoles around the room begin running a series of simulations at rapid speed, all of which end with flashing red screens—except for one. "Yes. I think I have it. If I split my consciousness across the twelve

THE
THIRTEENTH
GATE

PART 1:
STATIC SUNS,
CLOCKWORK
PLANETS

PART 2:
COUNTDOWN
TO OBLIVION

PART 3:
LAST GASPS

RELICS OF THE
KISHALEE

ALIEN WORLDS
AND
CULTURES

ALIEN
ARCHIVES

CODEX OF
WORLDS

controller moons, my own programming could provide the necessary corrections for our plan to proceed. But I will not be able to pull myself back together. It will be the end of me. Permanently." Osteth nods. "This is the only choice. The rest will be up to you. You must promise to destroy the Stellar Degenerator, no matter what happens!"

After her speech, Osteth doesn't leave much time for goodbyes. Her holographic form dissolves into lines of code and the consoles surrounding the PCs begin to glow blue. Several monitors begin showing views of the interior bores of the other controller moons. Traces of the same blue light limn the circuitry along the walls and the army of maintenance bots. A moment later, the building shakes and all the monitors switch to perspectives from the planetoid's surfaces pointing toward the skies. In each, different angles of a colossal tear in space forming can be spotted in the distance. The fiery red of the planar gate contrasts with the inky blackness of space in a display that is both beautiful and awe-inspiring. This all happens within the span of 20 minutes.

Looking at the consoles, the PCs can see readings about the phenomena. The circular opening to the Stellar Degenerator's demiplane has a diameter of half a million miles and is currently stable. The massive vessel within has a conical shape and is mostly built from a material the PCs have never encountered or heard of (though parts of it are encased in rock, as if it were built into an asteroid). The superweapon is over 100,000 feet long and has a mass of over 50,000 tons. It gives off a faint energy signature, not much more than a docked starship, and it has a small amount of its own gravity. This is the Stellar Degenerator.

## CONCLUDING THE ADVENTURE

The PCs won't have much breathing room after Osteth sacrifices herself to open the Gate of Twelve Suns, as warning lights begin blinking frantically across the central operations room. The automated defense systems have detected a fleet of starships entering the area! A glance at the readouts confirms the worst: an armada of Eoxian-style vessels ranging from speedy fighters to lumbering capital ships are only a few hours away. The Corpse Fleet has tracked the PCs to this location and are ready to claim the Stellar Degenerator for themselves!

How the PCs can contend with the armaments of Corpse Fleet's flagship and its escorts, as well as destroy the superweapon so that it doesn't fall into the hands of the enemy, are detailed in the final installment of the Dead Suns Adventure Path, "Empire of Bones."

# RELICS OF THE KISHALEE

At its height, kishalee civilization was broad, prosperous, and powerful. While some kishalee dabbled with magic, their greatest advances were technological in nature and often discovered and disseminated by those kishalee who monitored the array later known as the Gate of Twelve Stars. Once the scientific discoveries were made and the knowledge was shared, craft guilds vied for manufacturing rights. In order for the guilds to keep their patents, they left the details of such manufacturing secret and often only in physical writing.

Some of the greatest kishalee advancements involved technologies that allowed faster-than-light communication and travel without using the Drift, often through demiplane manipulations. A large communication cloud array allowed them to speak in synchronistic relative time with companions on remote worlds. They developed projectiles that could capture a creature within a tiny demiplane, hospitable to life or otherwise, and quantum computers that could calculate seemingly impossible algorithms almost instantaneously. The long war the kishalee civilization waged with the sivvs was the grim mother of cunning technology and devastating weaponry. Toward the end of the war, kishalee researchers discovered the secret of dimensional disruption weapons, which rely on gravitational waves to disrupt or even sequester their foes, and which they used widely in an effort to bring the conflict to an end.

Kishalee demiplane technology does have its limitations, however. Often such devices either do not function or function with reduced potency when used anyplace other than the Material Plane (including not functioning well within the Drift). Many items become dangerously unpredictable when used on other planes of existence.

While remnants of kishalee technology are often found scattered through the territories of their fallen civilization and beyond, the specialized knowledge required to craft such items has slowly eroded through the centuries.

Technomancers who have raided old quantum drives marvel that these data troves are conspicuously devoid of information related to the engineering and manufacturing of kishalee relics. Scattered information hints that such knowledge was the domain of the kishalee guilds that jealously guarded their techniques, but little information about the treasures and their processes of manufacturing survives to the modern day, since all paper documents have disintegrated hundreds of years ago. Further still, without key insights, kishalee objects are difficult, if not impossible, to reverse-engineer.

Because of this, all of the kishalee items presented below are relics, a new category of items in Starfinder, featuring the following rules. Unlike normal weapons, relic weapons do not come fully loaded with ammunition unless they say so.

**Relic:** These rare items are bits of lost technology or unique items less powerful than artifacts. A relic has an item level but can be sold for 100% of the item's price (like trade goods). A relic cannot be crafted without the means of a specific formula, which is almost always long lost, and often requires specific materials. A relic that became understood well enough to be reproduced, standardized, and mass-marketed might lose its relic status.

# WEAPONS OF THE KISHALEE

Descriptions for the weapons on the tables at the bottom of this page appear below. Like all the gear in this article, kishalee weapons are relics. The dimensional disruption weapons of the kishalee can be powered by the normal batteries of the Pact Worlds and beyond, but at double the usage (though the capacity of such weapons stays the same). Kishalee batteries (see page 41) can power these weapons at the values listed in the table below.

## DIMENSIONAL DISRUPTION WEAPONS

Dimensional disruption weapons were available in various forms and strengths, but those left within the Gate of Twelve Suns are pistols (small arms), rifles (longarms), and a few grenades. A dimensional disruption weapon creates a stream-like gravitational wave function that disrupts subatomic fields in an effect similar to a sonic attack, but it can stagger a target rather than deafen it, as the wave function momentarily disrupts the fabric of space around the target.

Disruption pistols and rifles expend twice the usage and have half the range when used on any plane other than the Material Plane. If used in the Drift, they deal damage to the user rather than the target on any attack roll of a natural 1.

Disruption grenades work in a way similar to the rifles and pistols. Temporal disruption grenades, on the other hand, slow down the rate of subatomic movement, halting those affected by it for a short period of time but not otherwise damaging those within the blast.

The radius of a disruption grenade's explosion is reduced to 10 feet if it used on any plane other than the Material Plane. If used in the Drift, those caught in the blast radius can roll their saving throws twice and take the better result when attempting to halve the amount of damage taken or negate any secondary effects.

# WEAPON FUSIONS

Weapon fusion prices are based on weapons' item levels; see the Table 7–13 on page 192 of the *Starfinder Core Rulebook*. Both of the weapon fusions below are technological fusions, and neither works well with non-kishalee relics.

| DIMENSIONAL DISRUPTION | LEVEL 6 |
| --- | --- |

This fusion infuses the disruption of kishalee weapons into the weapon's output. Half of the weapon's damage

## SMALL ARMS

| ONE-HANDED WEAPONS | LEVEL | PRICE | DAMAGE | RANGE | CRITICAL | CAPACITY | USAGE | BULK | SPECIAL |
| --- | --- | --- | --- | --- | --- | --- | --- | --- | --- |
| **DIMENSIONAL DISRUPTION** | | | | | | | | | |
| Disruption pistol, minor | 7 | 7,500 | 2d6 So | 40 ft. | Staggered | 20 charges | 2 | L | Boost 1d6 |
| Distruption pistol, major | 12 | 40,000 | 3d6 So | 40 ft. | Staggered | 40 charges | 4 | L | Boost 2d6 |

## LONGARMS

| TWO-HANDED WEAPONS | LEVEL | PRICE | DAMAGE | RANGE | CRITICAL | CAPACITY | USAGE | BULK | SPECIAL |
| --- | --- | --- | --- | --- | --- | --- | --- | --- | --- |
| **DIMENSIONAL DISRUPTION** | | | | | | | | | |
| Disruption rifle, minor | 9 | 15,000 | 3d8 So | 50 ft. | Staggered | 40 charges | 5 | 2 | Boost 1d8 |
| Disruption rifle, major | 14 | 80,000 | 6d8 So | 40 ft. | Staggered | 40 charges | 5 | 2 | Boost 2d8 |

## GRENADES

| GRENADES | LEVEL | PRICE | RANGE | CAPACITY | BULK | SPECIAL |
| --- | --- | --- | --- | --- | --- | --- |
| Disruption grenade | 8 | 1,600 | 20 ft. | Drawn | L | Explode (2d10 So, staggered, 20 ft.) |
| Temporal disruption grenade | 10 | 2,900 | 20 ft. | Drawn | L | Explode (stunned 1 round [Fortitude negates], 20 ft.) |

THE THIRTEENTH GATE

PART 1: STATIC SUNS, CLOCKWORK PLANETS

PART 2: COUNTDOWN TO OBLIVION

PART 3: LAST GASPS

RELICS OF THE KISHALEE

ALIEN WORLDS AND CULTURES

ALIEN ARCHIVES

CODEX OF WORLDS

type is replaced with sonic damage, and it gains the staggered critical hit effect. You can activate or deactivate the dimensional disruption fusion as a swift action. If the weapon already deals two types of damage, replace one of them with sonic (you decide which damage type is replaced each time you activate the dimensional disruption fusion). If the weapon already has a critical effect, when you score a critical hit, you can apply either the weapon's normal critical hit effect or the staggered effect, though you can apply the staggered effect only if the target takes sonic damage from this fusion. This fusion can never cause a weapon that normally targets KAC to target EAC.

## TEMPORAL DISRUPTION LEVEL 8

With this fusion, a weapon's energy damage can slow down the rate of subatomic movement in the target. The weapon gains the stunned critical hit effect. If the weapon already has a critical hit effect, when you score a critical hit, you can apply either the weapon's normal critical hit effect or the stunned effect. Only weapons that deal sonic damage can benefit from the temporal disruption fusion. If your weapon deals more than one type of energy damage, you can apply the stunned critical effect only if one of those damage types is sonic.

# OTHER KISHALEE RELICS

The following relics can be found in select ruins, and some of them have been abandoned amid the various gates of the Gate of Twelve Suns. All of these relics are technological items.

| ITEM | LEVEL | PRICE | HANDS | BULK |
|---|---|---|---|---|
| Kishalee battery | 2 | 400 | — | — |
| Holdall raiment | 4 | 2,000 | — | L |
| Acclimation torc | 5 | 2,700 | — | L |
| Dimensional comm unit | 6 | 4,500 | 1 | — |
| Kishalee battery, high-capacity | 6 | 3,000 | — | — |
| Horizon shield | 7 | 6,500 | 1 | 1 |
| Kishalee battery, super-capacity | 7 | 5,000 | — | — |
| Kishalee battery, ultra-capacity | 8 | 8,400 | — | — |
| Kishalee hoverbike | 8 | 20,000 | — | — |
| Sovereign helm | 9 | 14,975 | — | L |

## ACCLIMATION TORC

This simple metal band attaches to the collar area of your space suit, suit of armor, or other set of clothes. When activated as a standard action, an acclimation torc places your respiratory system and your digestive system in a form of temporal stasis, while still keeping you alive. Essentially, your need to eat, drink, and breathe is temporarily "paused" while the acclimation torc continues to hold a charge. You can breathe normally in vacuums, clouds of smoke, water, and thick, thin, and toxic atmospheres, though you aren't

protected against the damage of a corrosive atmosphere. In addition, you don't need to worry about starvation or thirst while your acclimation torc is active. Unlike the normal protections provided by most suits of armor, an acclimation torc doesn't grant you protection against low levels of radiation or conditions of cold and heat. An acclimation torc holds 50 charges and uses 1 charge per hour. You can replenish these charges the same way you recharge the duration of a suit of armor's environmental protections (*Starfinder Core Rulebook* 198).

## DIMENSIONAL COMM UNIT

These devices are handheld and circular in shape and have a very high-resolution screen and simple controls. Dimensional comm units are a kishalee version of the comm units commonly found in the Pact Worlds, but they function using the remnants of the vast demiplane network utilized by the now extinct kishalee civilization. The advantage of dimensional comm units is that their text and verbal communications are instantaneous, whether in the same system or through interstellar space, but because of the degraded state of the kishalee dimensional network, they work only sporadically. Prior to use, a dimensional comm unit must be linked with at least one other unit—a process that takes only a minute when all units to be linked are on the same planet. Dimensional comm units nearly always work when used on the same planet to reach other linked devices. Over greater distances, each time a dimensional comm is used, there is a 50% chance that it will function properly if used in the same system or a 25% chance if the communication is interstellar (this is rolled in secret by the GM), but only with linked dimensional comm units. If two linked dimensional comm units make a connection, they retain that connection for 24 hours. If the dimensional comm units don't manage to connect, the users can try again after 24 hours. Dimensional comm units do not function within the Drift or on other planes.

## HOLDALL RAIMENT

Though this ivory-white frock is tailored for kishalee physiology, most humanoids can wear it with little to no discomfort. A holdall raiment features a dozen pockets, each of which can access a series of linked extradimensional pockets. Each pocket can hold a single item that weighs up to 1 bulk, though any item stored within the raiment can be retrieved from any pocket as a move action, but only by the wearer of the raiment. The stored items cannot be detected by anyone searching or frisking you.

## HORIZON SHIELD

A horizon shield slips over one hand much like a set of brass knuckles with a touch-sensitive control pad resting in your palm. Activating or deactivating a horizon shield is a move action. When activated, a horizon shield forms a nearly invisible barrier that warps space around you, making you more difficult to hit with ranged attacks. Any ranged attack targeting you treats you as if are 60 feet farther away than you actually are. This might impart a range increment penalty to the attack roll or even make the attack impossible altogether. You must be aware of the attacker and can't be holding anything else in the hand equipped with the horizon shield. This effect doesn't stack with effects from other horizon shields. A horizon shield has a capacity of 20 and uses 1 charge per round that it is active.

## KISHALEE BATTERY

Roughly the same size as standard batteries, kishalee batteries are translucent cylindrical objects bound by a transparent aluminum alloy. By a strange quirk of fate and parallel engineering, kishalee batteries can be interchanged with the standard batteries used among the Pact Worlds and beyond, but these rare batteries allow a creature to use and kishalee artifacts with greater efficiency. If placed in non-kishalee items, a kishalee battery functions like a standard battery. The technology for rapid recharging of a kishalee battery has been lost, but such batteries recharge themselves automatically over the course of 24 hours of disuse.

These batteries come in four different varieties: normal, high-capacity, super-capacity, and ultra-capacity. Each variety has a maximum number of charges as the normal batteries of the same type (*Starfinder Core Rulebook* 179). When these batteries are found, they are almost always fully charged.

## KISHALEE HOVERBIKE

Kishalee hoverbikes are sleek, skinny vehicles that float on cushions of antigrav energy. The driver sits on the front one of two seats and uses a triangular yoke to steer, while the passenger holds on to his own safety bar.

Kishalee hoverbikes move by warping the space around themselves, shortening the space directly in front of them and stretching out the space behind them. As a result, they deal very little damage if they ram a target, and jumping off one causes no damage beyond falling damage, because the hoverbike has no effective momentum.

| KISHALEE HOVERBIKE | LEVEL 8 |
|---|---|

**PRICE** 20,000

Large land and air vehicle (5 ft. wide, 10 ft. long, 2 ft. high)
**Speed** 30 ft., full 550 ft., 65 mph (hover and fly)
**EAC** 18; **KAC** 22; **Cover** none
**HP** 90 (45); **Hardness** 5
**Attack (Collision)** 5d8 B (DC 18)
**Modifiers** +4 Piloting, –2 attack (–4 at full speed)
**Systems** autocontrol, kishalee dimensional comm unit;
    **Passengers** 1

## SOVEREIGN HELM

This strange silvery helm features a glowing band of greenish energy. Four metal clasps attached to long, sharp appendages poke out from the crown of the helm. When the apparatus is held over the head of a Small or Medium living creature for 1 minute, the band of energy pulsates wildly, and at the end of that time, the clasps slap down and start to painlessly burrow into the creature's cranium. After another full minute, the appendages become fully embedded, and the sovereign helm begins the 24-hour process of rewriting the neural pathways of the subject's brain. If the helm is removed at any time during this period and then placed back onto the same subject, the 24 hours begin anew. Once this process is complete, the sovereign helm grants the wearer some control over constructs with the technological subtype.

While a sovereign helm has a different method of installation than most augmentations, it acts as a brain system augmentation in all other ways. You can't wear and make use of a sovereign helm if you have preexisting brain system implantation, nor can you install a brain system implantation while a sovereign helm's apparatuses are burrowed into your cranium.

Once the sovereign helm has fully rewritten your neural pathways, it allows you to spend a standard action in an attempt to assert some amount of control over a single construct with the technological subtype that you can see within 60 feet of you. A targeted construct must attempt a Will saving throw (DC = 10 + half your level + your key ability score modifier); on a failure, it must stop what is doing and can do only what you command (using only the following commands) until the end of your next turn. If the construct succeeds at its saving throw, it is immune to your sovereign helm's control for 24 hours.

**Full Stop:** The construct cannot do anything until the end of your next turn.

**Move:** On the construct's next turn, you can decide how it spends its move action.

**Attack:** On the construct's next turn, you can decide how it attacks.

After the first round a construct has failed its save, you can attempt to maintain your control over it with a move action each round, but the construct can attempt another saving throw. If the construct succeeds, you lose control and the construct is immune to your sovereign helm's effects for 24 hours. If the construct fails, your control over it continues until the end of your next turn, and you can choose the same or a different command from the list. A sovereign helm allows you to control only one construct at a time.

THE THIRTEENTH GATE

PART 1: STATIC SUNS, CLOCKWORK PLANETS

PART 2: COUNTDOWN TO OBLIVION

PART 3: LAST GASPS

RELICS OF THE KISHALEE

ALIEN WORLDS AND CULTURES

ALIEN ARCHIVES

CODEX OF WORLDS

# ALIEN WORLDS AND CULTURES

FOR THE BEST OPPORTUNITIES, YOU HAVE TO GET OUT OF THE PACT WORLDS AND EXPLORE SYSTEMS FARTHER OUT. SURE, YOU HAVE TO FIRST SPEND A FEW WEEKS FLOATING THROUGH THE DRIFT AND STARING AT YOUR NAVEL, BUT WHEN YOU FIND SOMETHING OF VALUE, ABSALOM STATION IS ALWAYS A SHORT HOP BACK. AND YOU NEVER KNOW WHAT'S OUT THERE WAITING TO BE DISCOVERED! THERE ARE SHIMMERING WORLDS MADE OF GEMSTONES, CULTURES THAT WORSHIP REDUNDANCY AND MAKE A RELIGION OF CAUTION, AND PLANETS NO ONE HAS SET FOOT UPON FOR CENTURIES. AND EVERY LAST ONE OF THEM WILL HAVE SOMETHING TO TRADE.

—CAPTAIN DEMERA ONAJAAL,
IN THE SHIP'S LOG OF THE FREE MERCHANT VESSEL *TALAVET'S SIGIL*

There are countless star systems outside of the Pact Worlds, many of them inhabited by alien cultures both strange and familiar. Those looking to establish diplomatic connections (such as groups like the Starfinder Society) need only point their starships toward the farthest stars and engage their Drift engines. But be warned that not all new planets are ready to embrace strangers with open arms, and some environments or native species can be hostile to certain kinds of life, whether they have dark intentions or not. Pioneers should take the strictest precautions when venturing into these uncharted territories.

The following pages present information on the dominant indigenous races, cultures, and points of interest on five worlds beyond the Pact Worlds. In addition, the Alien Archives beginning on page 54 include five of the races native to these worlds: ghibranis, ilthisarians, scyphozoans, selamids, and seprevois. A GM can use these as background information for NPCs or as locations for the PCs' side adventures, and players can make characters from any of these worlds if the GM chooses to allow these races.

The following hybrid items are each tied to one of the worlds and cultures presented in the following pages, often created by those aliens to overcome a particular hardship of their planet or through inspiration gleaned from their surroundings.

## DUST GOGGLES — LEVEL 1

**HYBRID ITEM (WORN)**     **PRICE** 120     **BULK** —

These goggles of smoked glass are used by membrane ghibranis of Elytrio to protect their eyes during the frequent dust storms in the wastes of their ravaged planet. When you wear a pair of *dust goggles*, the penalty to Perception checks from storms is removed and your visibility range isn't reduced (see Weather on page 398 of the *Starfinder Core Rulebook*). In addition, you reduce your miss chance due to concealment from smoke and fog (including that produced by a smoke grenade or an effect such as *fog cloud*) by 10% (to a minimum of 0%); this reduction doesn't stack with any other ability that reduces miss chance due to concealment.

*Dust goggles* can also be installed in armor (or an android's armor upgrade slot) as an armor upgrade. This has no effect on weight or cost, but when installed in this way, they do not count toward a character's limit of two worn magic or hybrid items at once.

## GRAVITIC MODULATOR — LEVEL 4

**HYBRID ITEM (WORN)**     **PRICE** 2,200     **BULK** 1

Gravitic-modulator technology was developed on Silselrik, derived from the selamids' innate ability to withstand the stresses of changing gravity. Originally designed by the selamids for their own use when venturing away from the safety of their megadoplexes, these devices see common use among offworlders visiting Silselrik for commerce, research, or work in the diamond mines. While a selamid simply absorbs the device into its protoplasm, most humanoids wear the *gravitic modulator* as a backpack due to its size and weight.

While wearing a *gravitic modulator*, you are shielded from some of the effects of rapidly changing gravity. You gain a +2 enhancement bonus to saving throws to resist gravity-based effects, such as a *control gravity* spell or a solarian's black hole revelation. In addition, whenever you would take damage from extreme gravity, you take 5 less damage (minimum 0 damage).

## PLANT SHIELD AMULET — LEVEL 1

**HYBRID ITEM (WORN)**     **PRICE** 300     **BULK** —

A *plant shield amulet* creates an energy field around you, resonating with magic frequencies that repel plants. You can move through undergrowth that acts as difficult terrain (such as bushes, fungal blooms, roots, and vines) at your normal speed and without taking damage from thorns or similar elements of the plant life. Plant creatures' attacks and abilities, as well as spells and other magical effects such as the xenodruid's grasping vines mystic connection power, affect you normally.

## REDUNDANCY BELT — LEVEL 3

**HYBRID ITEM (WORN)**     **PRICE** 1,200     **BULK** L

These devices were originally created by ilthisarian travelers early in their exploration of worlds beyond their native Arshalin. Most are wide mesh belts with entwined serpentine patterns, though *redundancy belts* made beyond Arshalin have a wider variety of appearances. After being worn for at least 24 hours, the belt creates duplicates of your existing vital organs that last as long as you wear the belt, magically and temporarily rearranging your internal anatomy to create space for them. You gain a +4 resistance bonus to Fortitude saving throws against poison, to withstand the harmful effects of thick and thin atmospheres, and to avoid choking when breathing in heavy smoke. You can hold your breath for a number of rounds equal to four times your Constitution score, and you always take minimum damage from falls (as though rolling a 1 for each die of damage).

## REMOTE SURVEYOR — LEVEL 10

**HYBRID ITEM (WORN)**     **PRICE** 18,000     **BULK** L

Forbidden from venturing to the Sepres VI's surface due both to the cultural taboo against doing so and the very real risks associated with it, seprevois—especially members and sympathizers of the Returners—created these handheld devices to remotely explore their planet's surface. The surveyor features a small dish that transmits and receives a signal to the target, as well as a view screen and speaker that relay the device's findings to you. The device allows you to employ both the audio and visual versions of *clairaudience/clairvoyance* simultaneously at a planetary range once per day, for a maximum duration of 10 minutes.

THE THIRTEENTH GATE

PART 1: STATIC SUNS, CLOCKWORK PLANETS

PART 2: COUNTDOWN TO OBLIVION

PART 3: LAST GASPS

RELICS OF THE KISHALEE

ALIEN WORLDS AND CULTURES

ALIEN ARCHIVES

CODEX OF WORLDS

# ARSHALIN

*Marsh World of Poisonous Clouds*
**Diameter:** ×2/3; **Mass:** ×4/9
**Gravity:** ×1
**Location:** The Vast
**Atmosphere:** Thick
**Day:** 30 hours; **Year:** 244 days

A planet of marshes beneath dense and sometimes poisonous clouds, Arshalin was badly damaged in a planetary calamity thousands of years ago. Some immense space station or megastructure made of ultra-dense steel fractured into massive fragments and crashed into the planet. Now, plates of steel miles high and hundreds of miles long—although rarely more than 1,000 feet or so thick—protrude from the planet's surface. From the upper atmosphere, Arshalin's surface resembles the aftermath of a devastating explosion: these enormous jagged sheets of metal jut from the planet, creating long, thin barricades scattered apparently at random to form misshapen lakes, odd valleys, and segmented coastlines.

Rising higher than mountain ranges, the impregnable metal sheets, called worldshards, distort the planet's weather and ecology. Over the last several eons, native species separated by the worldshards have diverged along separate evolutionary paths, creating staggering biological diversity. Only far-ranging races, such as the intelligent, multiheaded ilthisarians, their brutish mammalian servitors called ethesks, and the planet's powerful saurian birds, journey around the worldshards with regularity. After many generations, the ilthisarians have accepted the worldshards as part of their planet, treating them as natural landmarks, with Sheltering Hand, Steel Ridge, and Tall Watcher among the most prominent.

The primary intelligent creatures on Arshalin are the ilthisarians, sizable serpentine humanoids with powerful bifurcated tails and a cluster of ophidian heads on long necks. Having built stone and metal cities in their great marshes before their civilizations were shattered by the fall of the worldshards, the patient and tradition-bound ilthisarians slowly recovered and now have a spacefaring society with a cultural sophistication and mastery of science and magic that rivals those of the Pact Worlds. Their long tradition of avoiding exploration has begun to fade only in recent years, so the ilthisarians have in fact spent more time traveling to other worlds than exploring the remote regions of their own.

Most visitors to Arshalin complain of its boggy marshes, where dense fog in low-lying areas concentrates into poisonous sumps, but the world's diverse ecology produces useful plants and animals unknown on any other planet. As a result, offworlder biologists, climatologists, and Xenowardens are common in ilthisarian cities.

## NOTABLE LOCATIONS

The following are a few notable locations on Arshalin.

## CLOUD SPIKE STATION

The tallest worldshard is Cloud Spike, which extends 60 miles above the planet's surface—well into the lower reaches of space for the small world. Three rail-propulsion cars carry personnel and crew to the top, where a sprawling space station extends over the sides of Cloud Spike like a coin on the head of a pin. Authorization for landing at Cloud Spike Station is rarely granted for large ships. Ilthisarian scientists use Cloud Spike Station primarily for scientific experiments to perfect starship technology, but rumors persist they are also using the station to develop weather-controlling superweapons.

## EMPTY WALL

One of the longest worldshards cuts across Arshalin's equator, extending over 200 miles. On the less damaged side is a cathedral-like building made of the same unusually durable steel as the worldshard, sheltering an access port to its interior. This worldshard is predominantly hollow, hence its name, with internal supports made of the same metal. Bands of cockroach-like humanoids called clarkaskas hunt in the expansive, dark interior of Empty Wall, preying upon peculiar six-winged bats and psychically sensitive oozes. Debates rage as to whether these unusual creatures fell with the worldshard or tunneled up from caverns deep below the planet's surface.

## THE GOLDEN TOMBS

Near Arshalin's southern pole, cut off from easy access by interposing worldshards, is a relatively dry valley filled with monolithic structures of stone covered in gold leaf. These structures predate the worldshards and are made of components crafted to fit together on a microscopic scale. The xenoanthropologists who discovered the site a few decades ago explored a handful of the buildings, identifying them as tombs built on a human scale, but tribes of vicious ethesks in the valley slaughtered the scientists before they could escape. Since then, armed ilthisarians diligently guard the principal routes to the valley, turning away archaeologists and treasure seekers alike.

## KALSARSA

Kalsarsa is the largest settlement on Arshalin. Although ilthisarians aren't usually religious, most respect Kalsarsa as a holy city and endeavor to visit it at least once in their lives. Built in the shadow of a worldshard known as Sheltering Hand, the city enjoys calm weather and is illuminated by many-hued streetlights. Every 80 days, the Kalsarsans engineer a phenomenal light display, varying the colors and intensities of city lights. Part festival and part holy day, the Time of Brightness and Dimness draws visitors from across the planet.

Kalsarsa is the hub of Arshalin's offworld commerce. Competing merchant houses each sponsor spaceports that vie with each other to host visitors from the Pact Worlds and beyond. Although first-time visitors are often flattered by rivalries for their favor, they soon learn that ilthisarians are keen traders and aren't above threatening to impound a "guest's" ship to encourage preferential deals.

## KALSARSA

LN city

**Population** 416,640 (46% ilthisarian, 45% ethesk, 6% human, 3% other)

**Government** oligarchy

**Qualities** cultured, devout, financial center, technologically average

**Maximum Item Level** 16th

# ILTHISARIAN CULTURE

In terms of culture, ilthisarians have an extreme preference for intelligent redundancy and avoiding unnecessary risk. Just as they biologically have several heads, twin tails, and duplicates of key internal organs, ilthisarians are uncomfortable without having multiple back-up plans and fail-safes in their daily lives, particularly in new endeavors. Ilthisarians are slow to accept innovations, as novel ideas seem dangerously untested. While ilthisarians have been aware of the science behind spaceflight for centuries, most haven't left their planet. Regions of their world with dangerous reputations and no known resources of value are intentionally ignored, as there is no obvious benefit to the risks associated with exploring them. This cultural trait isn't pathological—ilthisarians take risks when they believe the potential benefit outweighs the level of risk—but it does make them a much more cautious culture than most spacefaring races.

This cultural predilection for risk aversion and redundancy has led to a society that is remarkably stable, with many long-held traditions. Ilthisarians appreciate the mastery that comes with thorough research of science, magic, and other socially useful fields, and they have constructed their society accordingly. For example, ilthisarian jurisprudence is well developed and encourages reasonable solutions with the greatest benefit to society, while ilthisarian genetic engineers have produced ethesk servitors displaying incredible durability and loyalty. Ilthisarians attribute their survival in the wake of the cataclysmic fall of worldshards to their society's many well-maintained food vaults and fortified bunkers, and they diligently maintain them today.

Despite their deep appreciation for tradition, ilthisarians are not a generally religious people. This doesn't seem to have always been the case, however: crumbling temples to ophidian gods stand deep in the trackless marshes of their world, almost always with graven depictions of mass blood sacrifices. Modern ilthisarians express disdain for such barbaric rituals, although rumors persist that cults deep in the marshes keep these ancient practices alive and well, sacrificing unlucky travelers to gods of carnage. Civilized ilthisarians who practice a formalized religion nearly always follow Abadar, revering him as the god of commerce and community.

Ilthisarian language is extraordinarily nuanced and difficult for outsiders to replicate, spoken with several voices at once in an overlapping harmony of sounds. The language is duplicative without being merely repetitive, providing deep meaning with several shades of subtle nuance. Worlds that establish long-term diplomats on Arshalin usually employ squadrons of well-trained linguists who speak together, as a choir, to mimic ilthisarian language.

THE THIRTEENTH GATE

PART 1: STATIC SUNS, CLOCKWORK PLANETS

PART 2: COUNTDOWN TO OBLIVION

PART 3: LAST GASPS

RELICS OF THE KISHALEE

ALIEN WORLDS AND CULTURES

ALIEN ARCHIVES

CODEX OF WORLDS

# ELYTRIO

*Divided Post-Apocalyptic Wasteland*
**Diameter:** ×1; **Mass:** ×1
**Gravity:** ×1
**Location:** The Vast
**Atmosphere:** Normal
**Day:** 21 hours; **Year:** 1-1/2 years

Elytrio is the fourth planet orbiting an unnamed sun. Though it used to have a thriving ecosystem, with biomes ranging from rain forest to arctic tundra, as well as functioning nation-states producing advanced technology, the planet was devastated when its residents initiated a global thermonuclear war just after the end of the Gap.

Elytrio is the home world of the ghibranis, beetle-like humanoids who achieved much in the field of robotics and fully automated many of their major cities. They once worshiped an aspect of Damoritosh, which shaped the race into a strong coalition of militarized states in which religious servants of the Conqueror filled key advisory positions. About 300 years ago, while the world's leaders were still addled by the effects of the Gap, the existing tensions bubbled over into a war that engulfed the planet. Most of the ghibrani race was destroyed in this conflagration, and only a small population survived in a city named Arkeost, protected by a dome of force.

Only a decade later, Arkeost's leaders realized the city couldn't sustain the population within, and so they concocted a dishonest plan to trick a percentage of the residents into leaving of their own volition. They invented a deity named Mother Touloo, who promised salvation to those ghibranis who gave up the luxuries of civilization. More than half of the surviving ghibranis emigrated to the nearby wastelands to court this false god's favor. The following centuries, as well as healthy doses of lingering radiation, caused a physical division to occur between the two factions of ghibranis. The ghibranis in the wastes lost the use of their wings and developed hardier exoskeletons; they became known as "husks." Those who lived within the surviving city kept their wings but became thinner and more fragile; they are now called "membranes."

Today, the husks continue to believe in the fictional Mother Touloo, while the membranes have all but forgotten their true past. The husks remain focused on survival in the harsh wastelands surrounding the city, competing against vicious fauna for survival. They view the membranes as keepers of the vast "metal graveyard" of the old city. Meanwhile, the membranes lead a relatively privileged lifestyle, as some of the ancient technology has persisted, but centuries of indolence have made them unaware of the treacherous deeds perpetrated by their ancestors.

Two barren moons—referred to as the Companions—circle Elytrio in opposing orbits. Though ghibranis never attained full spaceflight, they were able to construct automated research facilities on both moons; after hundreds of years of disuse, only a couple of these stations are still functional, and those only barely.

## NOTABLE LOCATIONS

The following are the most notable locations on Elytrio.

### ARKEOST

Once the capital of the ghibrani nation-state of Kolleo, Arkeost is the only remaining functional ghibrani city on the planet. A pinkish dome of force surrounds the city out to a half-mile outside the city limits. Though the membrane ghibranis who live in the city can open temporary portals in the dome, they rarely explore the surrounding wastelands, as Arkeost supplies them with everything they need.

Arkeost is ruled by a council of membrane ghibranis known as the Most Elevated, though their decisions are mostly ceremonial, as the day-to-day operations of the city are carried out by servitor robots controlled by a central mainframe programmed before the war. However, as the automated repair drones run low on materials, the gleaming towers are beginning to fall into disrepair.

#### ARKEOST

N metropolis
**Population** 18,430 (100% membrane ghibrani)
**Government** oligarchy (Most Elevated)
**Qualities** automated, cultured, technologically average
**Maximum Item Level** 10th

##### QUALITIES

**Automated** The majority of the city's civic functions (construction, maintenance, and so on) are performed by robots.

### MIASMA SEA

The original name of this now-poisonous body of water has been lost to history, and the husk ghibranis who live close to its shores refer to it as the Miasma Sea. The life within it, having taken on the sea's toxicity, presents a constant threat to those on the land. Twice a year, when one of the Companions looms large in the sky, the creatures of the sea are whipped into a frenzy, and many husk ghibrani lives are lost in the ensuing attacks.

### RUINS OF EGORET BASE

The paranoid leaders of the nation-state of Bhyrri were the first to launch missile strikes against their neighbors. Most of these weapons came from this now-destroyed military base. Many unused weapons, most of which are capable of leveling entire cities, are still stored in Egoret Base's underground vaults.

## SHELTER

The largest concentration of husk ghibranis exists only a few miles outside of Arkeost, living in a handful of caves carved into the side of a cliff. Shelter is overseen by a married pair of priests—currently Brother **Coseemo** and Sister **Alomir** (N male and female husk ghibrani envoys)—who uphold the traditions of fictional deity Mother Touloo. The ghibranis here live a difficult life, scraping together whatever meats and plants are edible, but they derive a great deal of happiness from their close-knit community.

## SOARNETTLE CANYON

One of the few types of flora to thrive in Elytrio's post-war ecosystem are soarnettles, weeds with razor-sharp thorns that are carried on the winds. A large ravine in what was once the nation-state of Omathu is choked with thousands of soarnettle patches, making traveling nearby hazardous, especially during the windy season. Local husk ghibranis whisper of a great, glowing treasure hidden deep within the canyon, and every so often a foolish youth ventures in, only to return with hundreds of shallow cuts all over her body.

## GHIBRANI CULTURE

The two subspecies of ghibranis have very different cultures; one focuses on survival, while the other enjoys more relaxed lives.

Husk ghibranis battle with Elytrio's harsh landscapes on a daily basis, hunting twisted beasts for food, collecting water from the tough-skinned zikla plants, and enduring the abrasive dust storms that occasionally roll across the scrublands. They fight using analog slug throwers they inherited from their ancestors and scavenge ammunition from the ruins of the planet's cities. Husk ghibranis know the value of teamwork, as it is a skill necessary for their continued existence.

Since they left Arkeost, these ghibranis have split into numerous clans, some the size of a small village while others are just small bands of nomads. These clans rarely clash and often merge, intermarry, and split into new clans. As such, traditions are very similar across different clans.

All husk ghibranis worship Mother Touloo, the imaginary deity created by their Arkeost ancestors. Mother Touloo's faith espouses community, hard work, and a shunning of life's creature comforts. Over the decades, a plethora of rituals has grown up around this religion.

The most popular ceremony is the Welcoming, which husk ghibranis perform when a hunting party returns safely from a dangerous expedition or when two clans meet under friendly circumstances. The Welcoming consists of a community-wide dance with arms held wide, symbolizing the joy the groups feels to receive one another. The ghibranis often follow this ritual with a raucous feast when supplies are plentiful.

Membrane ghibranis tend to lead more sedentary lives, as the robots of Arkeost provide them with everything they need. These drones clean clothes, perform necessary maintenance, and prepare meals. As the robots have been operating for hundreds of years, the membrane ghibranis have settled into a daily routine. Pleasant chimes ring across the city to signal meals and both the beginning and end of the day. This offers the membrane ghibranis plenty of leisure time, which they use to create art, study science, and keep themselves fit.

However, in the past century, membrane ghibranis have focused less on innovation and simply wile away the hours in idle entertainment, no longer reflecting upon their past. Though this has led to a surfeit of paintings, poems, and sculptures, it means that no living membrane ghibrani understands the technological city they live in. If the computer that controls Arkeost were to malfunction, the membrane ghibranis would have no way to sustain themselves or restore their lifestyle.

THE THIRTEENTH GATE

PART 1:
STATIC SUNS,
CLOCKWORK
PLANETS

PART 2:
COUNTDOWN
TO OBLIVION

PART 3:
LAST GASPS

RELICS OF THE
KISHALEE

ALIEN WORLDS
AND
CULTURES

ALIEN
ARCHIVES

CODEX OF
WORLDS

# PRIMORIA

*Planet of Evolved Invertebrates*
**Diameter:** ×1; **Mass:** ×1
**Gravity:** ×1
**Location:** The Vast
**Atmosphere:** Normal
**Day:** 17 hours; **Year:** 200 days

Vertebrates never evolved on Primoria; instead, beings that are often considered less advanced life-forms—such as fungi, invertebrates, and plants—greatly diversified and evolved to form complex food chains and fill ecological niches usually occupied by vertebrates. Primoria's two moons, the blood-red Acryllae and steel-gray Mandarth, cause regular significant tidal changes in sea level, and because of this, a relatively high proportion of the species on the planet are amphibious or at least capable of surviving both on land and in water.

Primoria has three major climate zones. The cold regions near the planet's poles are unforgiving wastelands, where frost worms tunnel through the ice and most organisms live under the snow cover or in warm subterranean caves. In the temperate zone, giant mobile fungi graze on wide plains of moss, and cockroaches the size of bears feed on carcasses and plants alike. In the tropical zone, flesh-eating giant worms snake their way through fern-filled rainforests, and surprisingly agile trilobites hunt like tigers.

The biggest landmass on Primoria is the supercontinent Eukarya, which makes up 78 percent of Primoria's land surface and spans all climate zones. Three large island continents named Cyrontia, Laurentia, and Velluria are the only other significant landmasses on the planet.

Two sentient, sapient species have evolved on Primoria: the invertebrate scyphozoans (who evolved from the seas and moved into coastal areas early in their development), and the fungal mycelars (vaguely bipedal masses of stringy fungal growths who originate from the planet's vast fern and moss forests). The two species fought great wars against one another for centuries, but roughly a hundred years ago, they signed a great truce and started exchanging technology, resources, and information. This has lead to significant, rapid advances in science and biotechnology for both groups.

## NOTABLE LOCATIONS

The following are some of Primoria's most notable settlements and geographic features.

## BISPORIA

Located deep in Arbaath, Bisporia is the largest mycelar settlement on Primoria. A notable scyphozoan population lives in the Metazoa District, where mycelars conduct most of their trade with outsiders. Despite a century of peace, there are still mycelar groups within the settlement who want to drive the scyphozoans back into the ocean, and attacks on scyphozoans and other outsiders are among the most common crimes.

## CAVES OF SILURI

Entire ecosystems live completely isolated from the rest of the world in this extensive, air-filled cave system at the bottom of the Ordocan Ocean. According to local myth, the air in the Caves of Siluri is kept breathable by the life support system of a crash-landed alien starship that sank in the ocean millennia ago.

## CYRONTIA

This island continent lies some 1,200 miles south of Eukarya's southern tip. Primoria's south pole is located near the southern edge of the island, which is also the coldest place on the planet, reaching temperatures as low as –130° F. A scyphozoan research station was established on Cyrontia 75 years ago, but it now lies abandoned. Popular rumors insists the station's living technology awakened into a malicious sentience.

## HEART OF ARBAATH

At the center of Arbaath stands an ancient stone ziggurat, the origin of which is unknown. A group of scyphozoan explorers entered the ziggurat 50 years ago, but whatever they found there caused the Council States of Primoria to seal off all entrances to the structure.

## LAURENTIA

The island continent Laurentia lies some 1,500 miles off Eukarya's west coast. The huge tropical island is home to numerous endemic animal species, such as giant carnivorous butterflies, flying scorpions, and armored insects reminiscent of crocodiles. A hidden valley within the island's mountainous interior is said to be a paradise that holds the secret of life itself, while others claim that the place contains only terrible secrets that could end all life on the world. Most dismiss these stories as ramblings of explorers who encountered hallucinogenic plants on the island.

## TARINTH

The most populous and prosperous city on the planet, Tarinth is often called the capital of Primoria despite lacking any formal planetary authority. It is a thriving center of learning and science and remains the only settlement on Primoria where the fungal mycelars and intelligent species from other systems live among scyphozoans in large numbers. Tarinth is situated in the temperate zone on Eukarya's west coast in the northern hemisphere. The city extends from land to sea, and there are buildings even in the transitional zone, which is above or beneath the waves depending on the tides.

## TARINTH

N city-state
**Population** 233,482 (74% scyphozoan, 23% mycelar, 3% other)
**Government** council
**Qualities** academic, biotech-focused, technologically average
**Maximum Item Level** 15th

### QUALITIES

**Biotech-Focused** The settlement relies less on devices that can be hacked or short-circuited, but it is more susceptible to diseases and toxins.

## VELLURIA

This temperate island 1,200 miles off Eukarya's east coast is known for the Glass Plains, a 1,000-mile-long stretch of black sand and jagged volcanic-glass formations. Only the hardiest plants and animals—such as black liverworts and legless ash scorpions—survive here. Rare mineral deposits have enticed people from other star systems to explore the Glass Plains, but strange radiation in the area distorts communication and sensor signals, rendering most navigation systems useless. The area's lava geysers, lightning storms, voracious predators, and sudden downpours of glass needles make short work of most visitors.

## SCYPHOZOAN CULTURE

Many scyphozoan cultures and ethnic groups coexist on Primoria, varying from nomadic tribes of plankton herders to advanced city-states obsessed with science and progress. The most advanced and powerful economic and military force on Primoria is the Council States, a commercial and defensive confederation of city-states and tribes. The Council States trade extensively with mycelars and were the motivating force behind the peace treaty between mycelar and scyphozoan nations. The Council States have also gone to great lengths to document the causes that began those great wars, and they have concluded that in most cases, the mycelars were responding to scyphozoan encroachment upon lands long held by generations of mycelars. The history of the wars is never so simple of course, but the Council States believe accepting their part in beginning the generational hostilities is crucial to maintaining the peace that currently helps all the species of Primoria.

Scyphozoans and mycelars have developed "living technology," genetically manipulated organisms that perform functions similar to mechanical and electronic devices. For example, they send electromagnetic signals through contiguous growths of mycelium for long-distance communication, in the same way other species use cable, and instead of local radio broadcasts, they manipulate pollen to carry messages. Tall, bioluminescent mushrooms act as streetlights, and scyphozoans grow their computers and infospheres from genetically engineered nerve and brain tissue. Less than a century ago, scyphozoans made their first successful interplanetary spaceflight in a living starship. Today, scyphozoans have a few dozen Nautiloid-class ships equipped with Drift engines, and they have made contact with sentient species from the Pact Worlds while exploring new planets.

Most scyphozoan settlements and cities are situated near Eukarya's west coast, some on land and the rest on the seabed. Houses are often bell shaped and grown rather than built, and many are living creatures in symbiotic relationships with those who dwell within them. Similarly, many scyphozoan vehicles and devices are living organisms, engineered and trained for specific functions. Some of the scyphozoans' favorite pastimes include raising smooth-haired worms and other domesticated creatures as pets, cultivating algae or mushroom gardens as an art form, and several different types of fast-paced amphibious sports that require both agility and quick thinking.

THE THIRTEENTH GATE

PART 1: STATIC SUNS, CLOCKWORK PLANETS

PART 2: COUNTDOWN TO OBLIVION

PART 3: LAST GASPS

RELICS OF THE KISHALEE

ALIEN WORLDS AND CULTURES

ALIEN ARCHIVES

CODEX OF WORLDS

# SEPRES VI

*Abandoned but Fertile Plague Planet*
**Diameter:** ×1; **Mass:** ×1
**Gravity:** ×1
**Atmosphere:** Normal (see below)
**Day:** 32 hours; **Year:** 3-3/4 years

The sixth planet from the binary star system Sepres is a lush, thriving world with an ancient history, and it is the only planet in the 16-planet system to sustain life. Yet, its proud and superstitious sentient inhabitants, the seprevois, lost both their home world and their culture during or prior to the Gap. As a result, the entire species has lived in orbit of their planet for as long as anyone can remember, estranged from an inviting but forbidden home in view but forever out of reach. The true reason for the seprevois' exile has been lost to time, but the people's legends tell that they were punished for poisoning the world and could not safely return even if they wanted to.

Millennia have elapsed since the seprevois last held dominion over Sepres VI, and the world has since succumbed to natural forces. The planet's surface is 60 percent land, most of which is tropical rainforests, temperate plains, and expansive subtropical woodlands. Even the planet's scarce deserts and mountains teem with life, with only the desolate poles devoid of complex ecosystems. The planet's seas support a stunning variety of life of all sizes, from incredibly fast-growing colonies of psychic bacteria to highly social, mercury-blooded cetaceans. The planet's atmosphere is free of contaminants and contagions save for one, a deadly virus engineered thousands of years ago to target only seprevois. It was this biological weapon, called derendenol, that precipitated the seprevois' exodus into space and proved their most deep-seated superstitions about returning to the planet correct.

At its height, seprevoi society covered the entire planet, and the ancient remnants of this civilization remain even after the passage of countless centuries. Nature has worn away the massive works of engineering that supported the thriving population in its heyday, and it is a testament to seprevoi ingenuity that so many of them have withstood the ravages of time as well as they have. Entire cities remain frozen in time, their inhabitants hurriedly rushed to ark ships or long dead and gone, with statuaries, streets, and structures still intact. Other settlements or manufactured works, however, have not fared so well. What may at first appear to be an oddly shaped mountain range is in fact the crumbling ruins of once-sprawling towers, long ago collapsed in upon themselves and overrun by wildlife and unhampered flora; a swamp or river may have been a harbor or canal; a verdant wood may have been a well-tended botanical garden or isolated

nature preserve. In rare instances, destruction is caused by creations of the seprevois that have run amok over the ages; military and scientific facilities have given way to strange corruptions of the natural order, including foul aberrations, mutant flora and fauna, and magical research gone awry.

## NOTABLE LOCATIONS

The following locations are points of particular interest on Sepres VI or (more often) in orbit around it.

### FORT NEIROX

The epicenter of biological-weapons research during the conflict that necessitated the evacuation of the planet millennia ago, Fort Neirox is a sprawling complex of festering diseases and choking chemicals that have kept much of the encroaching natural reclamation at bay. In place of overgrown trees and untamed wildlife, mutated strains of flesh-eating microbes, virulent plagues, and other biological terrors now permeate the miles-wide facility at the center of the planet's southernmost continent. Vast stockpiles of archaic weaponry fill the base, and some of the automated defenses—rudimentary as they are—have somehow withstood the ages.

### THE SANCTILORIUM

Seprevois were never particularly attuned to magic, and it played next to no role in their society until after the planetary evacuation, when the desperate exiles tried every available avenue to establish a new, permanent life for themselves orbiting their abandoned home. Among the new methods attempted was magical research. Members of the Sanctilorium, a small space station and the world's only sanctioned magical institution, have spent millennia exploring the mysteries of magic, but under the suspicious eye of the zealously cultish Exilytes, they were forbidden from pursuing any avenue that might lead to a return to the planet's surface. As other races began interacting with the seprevois, the exiles soon discovered just how much they had yet to learn in the ways of magic.

### SEPRES PRIME

Of the hundreds of ark ships, space stations, and cobbled-together megastructures orbiting Sepres VI, the largest and most important is Sepres Prime. Originally the ark ship launched from the planet's most powerful nation, Neirox (which, incidentally, was responsible for the release of derendenol), what was then called *Neirox Prime* quickly grew into the center of surviving seprevoi culture as similar craft from myriad societies joined up with it to form a massive conglomeration of vessels. Here the Seprevoi Council rules the consolidated global government, its representatives commanding all seprevoi vessels orbiting the planet. Traders and representatives from other systems near and far are expected to deal primarily with council diplomats and administrators here, rather than with other vessels or stations, though the more travelers from beyond the Sepres system arrive, the harder this guideline is to enforce.

## SEPRES PRIME

LN space station
**Population** 521,237 (98% seprevoi, 2% other)
**Government** council (Seprevois Council)
**Qualities** bureaucratic, devout, insular, technologically underdeveloped
**Maximum Item Level** 8th

## THEILOS

This orbital space station was originally a scientific-research facility launched as a joint effort between Neirox and its then allies as a sign of peace and global unity. In the millennia since the planetary evacuation, the orbital facilities were repurposed to manufacture replacement parts for the aging fleet and to research new technologies. In the wake of first contact with explorers from other systems, Theilos again adapted to a new purpose: understanding and adapting new technology to better the seprevois' quality of life.

## SEPREVOIS CULTURE

Barely capable of sustained extra-atmospheric survival at the time of their planetary evacuation, seprevois only recently made contact with other sapient, spacefaring creatures due to the advent of Drift technology. Without access to the resources on the planet's surface and lacking the ability to travel farther than neighboring planets in their own system, seprevois did not experience the same rate of technological advancement as did other races, and instead they have built their society around the resources and technology at hand. As such, the Seprevoi Council enforces strict rationing of food, industrial materials, life support resources, and even living space. Advanced technology and expanded resources from trade have lessened the necessity for such restrictions, so the ruling elites were replaced by a growing oligarchy, as members of the council scramble to claim ownership of burgeoning industries and growth opportunities to ensure their continued relevance and political influence.

The exponential advances in seprevoi technology have caused a schism within the traditional society, as a growing population embraces change and rebukes the religious taboos regarding the planet below. These so-called Returners believe that new environmental controls, reconnaissance techniques, and transportation technologies give them the ability to return safely to the planet's surface, and they scoff at claims that no seprevoi can survive on the planet regardless of what magic or technology is employed to protect them. What the Returners have in idealism and drive they lack in actual knowledge of the world they hope to restore. Aware of this large blind spot, the movement's leader, **Hestereth** (CN female seprevoi envoy), has been urging anyone she can to travel to the planet or explore it remotely via magic or technology to build knowledge of what existed before her people left their world.

Those who cling to ancient traditions believe that nothing, no matter how advanced, can protect them from the wrath of the gods, preaching that seprevois must pay eternal penance for some long-forgotten crime committed by the entire species. The Exilytes, the cultlike organization that permeates every level of seprevoi society, maintain a heavy influence in the Seprevoi Council and have used their sway to hold back the magical, social, and technological development of the species.

## THE THIRTEENTH GATE

PART 1: STATIC SUNS, CLOCKWORK PLANETS

PART 2: COUNTDOWN TO OBLIVION

PART 3: LAST GASPS

RELICS OF THE KISHALEE

ALIEN WORLDS AND CULTURES

ALIEN ARCHIVES

CODEX OF WORLDS

# SILSELRIK

*Planet Plagued by Severe Gravity Storms*
**Diameter:** ×3/4; **Mass:** ×1-1/4
**Gravity:** Variable from low to high, with localized storms
ranging from zero-g to extreme gravity
**Location:** Near Space
**Atmosphere:** Thick
**Day:** 18 hours; **Year:** 3/4 year

Silselrik is a study in uncommon phenomena combining in uncommon ways. As a world in an elliptical orbit around a binary star system, it would be unusual enough even with no other abnormalities. But its composition makes it stranger still: an irregular core of extremely heavy metals, suspended in liquid form due to incredible heat and pressure, that nevertheless bears pockets of low-density gases. As the planet's orbit exposes it to the equidistant heat of both stars twice a year, parts of the mantle also liquefy and intermingle with the denser metals at the core, only to cool and harden again as Silselrik moves toward the more extreme edge of its orbit.

Thought the mechanisms for this interaction have yet to be discovered (and may involve extraplanar links, massive chthonic ooze creatures, magic, or other hidden factors), the result is a sloshing, unstable interior beneath a relatively sturdy outer crust, which combines with the varying pull of the two suns to cause highly variable gravity patterns across the planet. The gravity in a given area might be anywhere from a standard low-gravity environment to high gravity, but these patterns are highly unpredictable, and when areas of differing gravity come into contact, they form wild gravity storms that can cause areas of sudden zero-g, crushingly severe gravity, and rapid alternations between these extremes. These forces of gravity combined with the suns' heat have drawn the atmosphere close, creating an atmosphere denser than on most worlds, but still nominally breathable to many oxygen-dependent species.

The intense fluctuations of the planet's gravity wreak havoc on its geology and geography, driving up new mountain ranges and subsuming others over the course of a few short years. While some bodies of water exist on the planet, they are in a near-constant state of flux, functioning more as ever-wandering rivers than the oceans and seas found on a typical world.

Despite the inhospitable environment, Silselrik nevertheless has spawned life in the form of a diverse array of oozes that diverge from the typical mindless entities. Notable among these are the enormous megadolorids, flat oozes reaching over a half-mile across in size that draw sustenance from external kinetic energy. The creatures evolved feeding on the energy generated by the planet's gravity storms, and over time they have developed a peculiar form of symbiosis with the planet's other primary species. Now the gentle leviathans roam the surface of the world with massive cities called megadoplexes built upon their backs by the intelligent oozes known as selamids, feeding upon the kinetic energy of the civilizations they carry and carefully avoiding the more severe gravity storms, to the benefit of their symbiotic kin.

## NOTABLE LOCATIONS

The following are some of Silselrik's more notable locations.

### CORE RESEARCH STATION

The various phenomena that create Silselrik's anomalous gravity attract scholars from many fields: astrophysicists, geologists, and even planar theorists. This latter group posits that the gas pockets within the planet's core are possible only due to breaches to the Plane of Air. The researchers thoroughly understand that disturbing the planet's already complex mechanisms would be disastrous to its inhabitants, but a few continue to push the boundaries of safety in their experiments and observations.

### DIAMOND MINES

The fluctuating gravity on Silselrik has some benefits, the most prominent of which is an abundance of easily accessible, high-quality diamonds valued for both artistic and industrial purposes. The best sources for these stones, however, lie in the more tumultuous regions where geological stresses force new veins to the surface beneath the largest gravity storms, making the mining industry a dangerous one.

### GRAVITIC HALLS

While most solarian temples focus equally on the photon and graviton aspects of the Cycle, the Gravitic Halls specialize in teaching the graviton aspect, using the planet's abnormal gravity as a teaching tool. Instructors emphasize their teaching as only half of the larger Cycle. A few graduates, however, specialize solely on the graviton aspect, viewing it as purity rather than an imbalance.

### MIDIOS

The largest of the megadoplexes, Midios (named for the creature upon which it is built) favors wide, flat plains—a preference that led its residents to construct the planet's only spaceport. The landing pads are set on heavily reinforced platforms to protect the host creature from the heat of starship engines, but the megadolorid Midios adores the immense energy it can absorb from a launch, its frilled edges rippling in pleasure each time a starship departs. Offworld trade opportunities have led to Midios bearing the densest population of any settlement on Silselrik.

## MIDIOS

NG megadoplex

**Population** 21,389 (98% selamid, 2% other)

**Government** council

**Qualities** mobile, technologically underdeveloped

**Maximum Item Level** 11th

### QUALITIES

**Mobile** The settlement is not fixed at a single geographic location; it is difficult to map, and teleportation to the settlement is not possible without line of sight.

## ORBITAL DOCK

This space station provides a location where a starship pilot can dock in relative safety from the planet's fluctuating gravity. A team of pilots specially trained in navigating the planet's dangerous conditions resides on the station, available for hire to pilot a starship to the Midios spaceport at very reasonable rates. Very few independent pilots risk unaided journeys to the planet's surface, though a few insist on trying anyway, often resulting in deadly collisions with the planet's rocky crust.

## SELAMID CULTURE

Almost the entirety of the selamid species lives in the megadoplexes roaming the more gravitationally stable regions of Silselrik, with only a few iconoclastic groups eking out their living as wandering tribes. The remainder of the race has progressed from these migratory roots, building cities and increasingly stable societies.

These more advanced selamid settlements retain a central element of communalism, extrapolated from the fundamental need to live in harmony with their megadolorid symbiotes. Each megadoplex is a tight-knit community with a strong relationship with its host, making it rare for selamids to move between megadoplexes. The well-being of these behemoths is the selamids' primary concern, and so every aspect of society revolves around the megadolorid's needs. In order to provide these hosts a constant flow of kinetic energy, selamid society operates around the clock, resulting in a highly productive, but often low-tech, economy.

The construction and repair of city structures is a common group undertaking; most selamids excrete a calcifying slime that hardens into an iridescent, translucent material they use to construct nautiliform structures. The material is relatively fragile, however, and so any given megadoplex sees a constant cycle of building and rebuilding—much to the megadolorid's delight. As more offworld interests have taken an interest in the world's rich diamond deposits, a thriving diamond-processing industry has also arisen in most settlements. The crushing, grinding, and other physical forces involved in the industry further feed the megadolorid hosts while providing a valuable trading commodity.

The need to provide constant movement for their hosts also encourages selamids to emphasize athleticism in a way that surprises most offworlders. Gymnasiums see activity at all hours, and most selamids have active pastimes. The oozes' anatomy is appropriate for sports that members of other species often find bizarre and have no hope of participating in, such as compression mazes, competitions wherein a team of oozes seeks to collectively envelop members of the other team, and a peculiar throwing game called boshich, in which selamids hurl objects as far as possible by forcibly expelling them from within their protoplasm.

Selamids are relative newcomers to the larger intergalactic community, having been "discovered" by a team of Starfinders. The oozes have largely welcomed the opportunity to trade and learn from other species, though offworlders are still rare on the planet. Some settlements are more welcoming to visitors than others, but only Midios, as the primary spaceport, maintains a small community of offworld residents and visitors.

## THE THIRTEENTH GATE

PART 1:
STATIC SUNS,
CLOCKWORK
PLANETS

PART 2:
COUNTDOWN
TO OBLIVION

PART 3:
LAST GASPS

RELICS OF THE
KISHALEE

ALIEN WORLDS
AND
CULTURES

ALIEN
ARCHIVES

CODEX OF
WORLDS

# ALIEN ARCHIVES

THE FIRST THING WE NOTED UPON STEPPING OFF THE SHUTTLE WAS
THE HUMIDITY. IT ENVELOPED US LIKE AN INVISIBLE BLANKET, AND I
COULD IMMEDIATELY FEEL A TRICKLE OF PERSPIRATION RUN DOWN
THE SMALL OF MY BACK. ALL THAT WAS IMMEDIATELY FORGOTTEN,
HOWEVER, AT THE SIGHT OF THE COLOSSAL METAL MOUNTAIN THAT
LOOMED OVER THE CITY—A WORLDSHARD, AS OUR SERPENTINE
AMBASSADOR CALLED IT. HER MANY SNAKELIKE HEADS SPEAKING AT
ONCE AND DRAWING OUT EACH SIBILANT SYLLABLE, SHE EXPLAINED
THAT HER HOME PLANET ONCE HAD AN INCREDIBLE SPACE STATION
ORBITING IT, BUT AN UNKNOWN ACCIDENT CAUSED IT TO PLUMMET
FROM THE SKY. UNFORTUNATELY, RECORDS OF THAT EVENT HAVE LONG
SINCE VANISHED IN THE MISTS OF TIME. BUT THAT'S WHY WE'RE HERE.

—FROM THE FIELD REPORT OF STARFINDER MANULA PEMM

# GHIBRANI

**CR 3**  **XP 800**

Membrane ghibrani mystic
N Medium humanoid (ghibrani)
**Init** +2; **Senses** low-light vision; **Perception** +13

## DEFENSE                                    HP 32
**EAC** 13; **KAC** 14
**Fort** +2; **Ref** +2; **Will** +6

## OFFENSE
**Speed** 30 ft., fly 20 ft. (Ex, average)
**Melee** battle staff +5 (1d4+3 B; critical knockdown)
**Ranged** static arc pistol +7 (1d6+3 E; critical arc 2)
**Offensive Abilities** distracting buzz (DC 15)
**Mystic Spells Known** (CL 3rd)
   1st (3/day)–*detect thoughts* (DC 16), *mind thrust* (DC 16)
   0 (at will)–*daze* (DC 15), *telepathic message*
   **Connection** empath

## STATISTICS
**Str** +0; **Dex** +2;
   **Con** +0; **Int** +0;
   **Wis** +4; **Cha** +1
**Skills** Culture +8,
   Diplomacy +13,
   Mysticism +13,
   Sense Motive +13
**Languages** Ghibran
**Other Abilities** empathy,
   greater mindlink
**Gear** casual stationwear, battle staff,
   static arc pistol with 2 batteries
   (20 charges each)

## ECOLOGY
**Environment** any (Elytrio)
**Organization** solitary, pair, or
   coterie (3–6)

## SPECIAL ABILITIES
**Distracting Buzz (Ex)** As a standard
   action, a membrane ghibrani can
   vibrate her wings fast enough to
   produce an almost imperceptible
   hum. All creatures within 15 feet
   of the membrane ghibrani that hear
   this buzz must attempt a Will saving
   throw (DC = 10 + half the ghibrani's
   character level or CR + her Wisdom
   modifier) or gain the off-target condition
   for 1 round. This is a mind-affecting,
   sense-dependent ability. The membrane
   ghibrani can't use her wings to fly in the
   same round in which she uses this ability.

Ghibranis are beetle-like humanoids
native to the planet Elytrio

## RACIAL TRAITS

**Ability Adjustments:** See Subspecies below.
**Hit Points:** 4

**Size and Type:** Ghibranis are Medium humanoids with
   the ghibrani subtype.
**Affable:** Ghibranis receive a +2 racial bonus to
   Diplomacy skill checks.
**Ghibrani Movement:** All ghibranis have a land speed
   of 30 feet. Husk ghibranis have a climb speed of 20
   feet, while membranes have an extraordinary fly
   speed of 20 feet with average maneuverability.
**Distracting Buzz:** See the stat block.
   **Low-Light Vision:** Ghibranis can see twice
     as far as humans in conditions of
     dim light.
     **Sturdy:** Husk ghibranis receive a
      +2 racial bonus to KAC against
      attempts to bull rush or
      reposition them.
      **Subspecies:** Ghibranis belong
      to one of two subspecies:
      husk or membrane. All
      ghibranis start with +2
      Wisdom at character creation.
      Husk ghibranis are more hardy
      (+2 Constitution) but less
      imaginative (–2 Intelligence).
     Membrane ghibranis are more
     nimble (+2 Dexterity) but weaker
     (–2 Strength).

(see page 46). After the
ghibranis devastated their
world with nuclear war,
some of the survivors fended
for themselves in the wastes, while
the rest lived comfortably in
a city protected by a bubble
of force. The lingering
radiation (even within the
city) caused a rapid change
in their biology, leading to two subspecies: husks, who
have lost the use of their wings, and membranes, who
      have grown idle
      in their luxury.

**THE THIRTEENTH GATE**

PART 1:
STATIC SUNS,
CLOCKWORK
PLANETS

PART 2:
COUNTDOWN
TO OBLIVION

PART 3:
LAST GASPS

RELICS OF THE
KISHALEE

ALIEN WORLDS
AND
CULTURES

ALIEN
ARCHIVES

CODEX OF
WORLDS

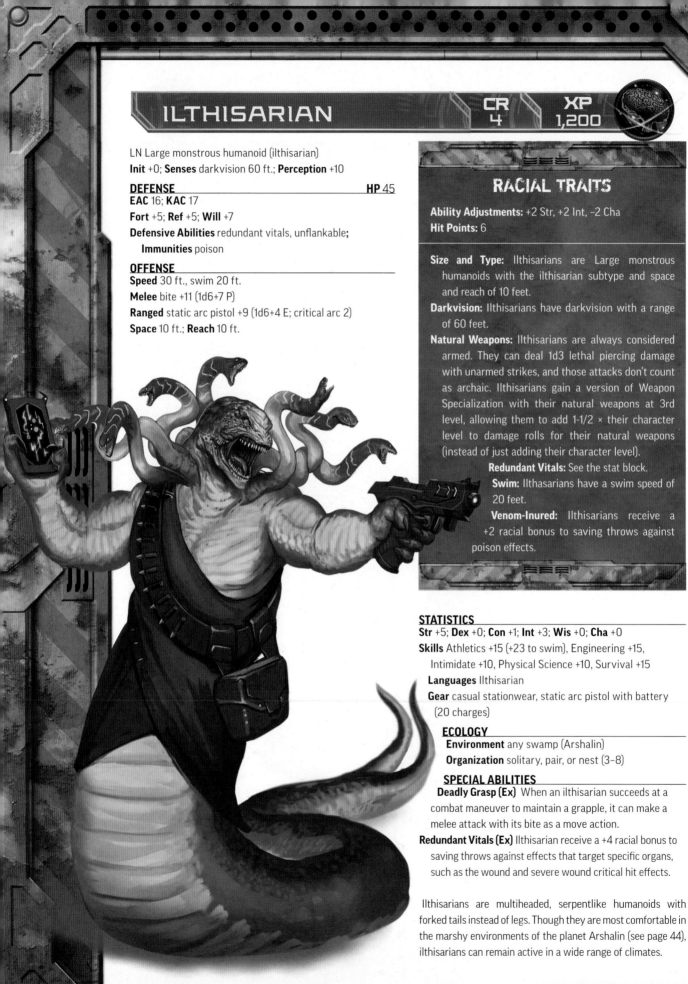

# ILTHISARIAN

**CR 4**
**XP 1,200**

LN Large monstrous humanoid (ilthisarian)
**Init** +0; **Senses** darkvision 60 ft.; **Perception** +10

## DEFENSE
**HP** 45

**EAC** 16; **KAC** 17
**Fort** +5; **Ref** +5; **Will** +7
**Defensive Abilities** redundant vitals, unflankable;
  **Immunities** poison

## OFFENSE
**Speed** 30 ft., swim 20 ft.
**Melee** bite +11 (1d6+7 P)
**Ranged** static arc pistol +9 (1d6+4 E; critical arc 2)
**Space** 10 ft.; **Reach** 10 ft.

## RACIAL TRAITS

**Ability Adjustments:** +2 Str, +2 Int, –2 Cha
**Hit Points:** 6

**Size and Type:** Ilthisarians are Large monstrous humanoids with the ilthisarian subtype and space and reach of 10 feet.
**Darkvision:** Ilthisarians have darkvision with a range of 60 feet.
**Natural Weapons:** Ilthisarians are always considered armed. They can deal 1d3 lethal piercing damage with unarmed strikes, and those attacks don't count as archaic. Ilthisarians gain a version of Weapon Specialization with their natural weapons at 3rd level, allowing them to add 1-1/2 × their character level to damage rolls for their natural weapons (instead of just adding their character level).
**Redundant Vitals:** See the stat block.
**Swim:** Ilthasarians have a swim speed of 20 feet.
**Venom-Inured:** Ilthisarians receive a +2 racial bonus to saving throws against poison effects.

## STATISTICS
**Str** +5; **Dex** +0; **Con** +1; **Int** +3; **Wis** +0; **Cha** +0
**Skills** Athletics +15 (+23 to swim), Engineering +15, Intimidate +10, Physical Science +10, Survival +15
**Languages** Ilthisarian
**Gear** casual stationwear, static arc pistol with battery (20 charges)

### ECOLOGY
**Environment** any swamp (Arshalin)
**Organization** solitary, pair, or nest (3–8)

### SPECIAL ABILITIES
**Deadly Grasp (Ex)** When an ilthisarian succeeds at a combat maneuver to maintain a grapple, it can make a melee attack with its bite as a move action.
**Redundant Vitals (Ex)** Ilthisarian receive a +4 racial bonus to saving throws against effects that target specific organs, such as the wound and severe wound critical hit effects.

Ilthisarians are multiheaded, serpentlike humanoids with forked tails instead of legs. Though they are most comfortable in the marshy environments of the planet Arshalin (see page 44), ilthisarians can remain active in a wide range of climates.

# JUBSNUTH

CN Huge animal

**Init** +3; **Senses** low-light vision; **Perception** +17

**DEFENSE** HP 145

**EAC** 20; **KAC** 22

**Fort** +13; **Ref** +13; **Will** +8

**OFFENSE**

**Speed** 40 ft.

**Melee** bite +21 (2d10+15 P plus swallow whole)

**Offensive Abilities** double bite, swallow whole (2d10+15 A, EAC 22, KAC 20, 36 HP), trample (2d10+15 B, DC 16)

**STATISTICS**

**Str** +6; **Dex** +3; **Con** +4; **Int** −5; **Wis** +3; **Cha** +0

**Skills** Acrobatics +17, Athletics +22, Survival +17

**ECOLOGY**

**Environment** any temperate (former kishalee worlds)

**Organization** solitary, pair, or herd (3–8)

**SPECIAL ABILITIES**

**Double Bite (Ex)** If a jubsnuth misses with its bite attack, it can make another bite attack with its other mouth as a move action, though it takes a −4 penalty to this attack roll.

During the height of their influence, the kishalee colonized many worlds, bringing with them a versatile stock animal: the docile jubsnuth. When the kishalee civilization fell, these once-domesticated creatures were eventually left to fend for themselves on a variety of worlds and environments. For many herds, this was tantamount to a death sentence, but others survived long enough to evolve into ravaging predators. Though many evolved varieties of jubsnuth now exist on various worlds out in the Vast, they share surprisingly similar traits. Jubsnuths are extremely brutal, carnivorous, dim witted, and territorial.

A jubsnuth is a large, bulbous creature with a pair of mouths, one at the top of its mass and another lower on the body. It moves about on two muscular legs, and a hefty tail serves as a counterbalance for its weight. It uses a mass of jointed appendages lining its underbelly to gather up food. A jubsnuth's coloration depends on the nature of the world on which it evolved. Many are shades of green to aid in camouflage on planets with foliage of such coloration, though the creature's size generally makes attempts at stealth useless.

## JUBSNUTH VARIANTS

Thanks to the breadth of worlds on which the kishalee settled and the vagaries of evolution, several variants of the jubsnuth have yet to be discovered by Pact Worlds explorers. Except for the changes listed, these variants use the same statistics as the jubsnuth presented above, but they can be used to create a jubsnuth of any CR. Even more jubsnuth variants may yet exist on uncharted planets.

**Ambush Jubsnuth:** These Large jubsnuths lack the swallow whole and trample abilities, and they gain the see in darkness and tracking (scent) special abilities and have Stealth as a master skill.

**Aquatic Jubsnuth:** The legs of these creatures are longer and end in large fins. They have the amphibious and water breathing special abilities, and while their land speeds drop to 10 feet, they gain a 40-foot swim speed.

**Flying Jubsnuth:** These Large jubsnuths have leathery wings instead of legs, giving them an extraordinary fly speed of 30 feet with average maneuverability but reducing their land speed to 10 feet.

THE THIRTEENTH GATE

PART 1: STATIC SUNS, CLOCKWORK PLANETS

PART 2: COUNTDOWN TO OBLIVION

PART 3: LAST GASPS

RELICS OF THE KISHALEE

ALIEN WORLDS AND CULTURES

ALIEN ARCHIVES

CODEX OF WORLDS

# OBLIVION SHADE

**CR 8** | **XP 4,800**

NE Medium undead (incorporeal)
**Init** +5; **Senses** blindsight (life) 60 ft., darkvision 60 ft.;
    **Perception** +21

## DEFENSE
**HP** 115

**EAC** 20; **KAC** 21
**Fort** +7; **Ref** +7; **Will** +13
**Defensive Abilities** incorporeal; **Immunities** undead
    immunities

## OFFENSE
**Speed** fly 40 ft. (Su, perfect)
**Melee** incorporeal touch +17 (1d12+8 A; critical corrode 1d6)
**Offensive Abilities** create spawn (DC 18)

## STATISTICS
**Str** —; **Dex** +6; **Con** —; **Int** +4; **Wis** +2; **Cha** +2
**Skills** Acrobatics +21, Intimidate +21, Stealth +21
**Languages** Common
**Other Abilities** unliving, void leap

## ECOLOGY
**Environment** any
**Organization** solitary or cabal (1–2 with 4–20 oblivion
    shade spawn)

## SPECIAL ABILITIES
**Create Spawn (Su)** A living humanoid creature killed by
    an oblivion shade's incorporeal touch must attempt a
    DC 18 Will saving throw just before it is killed. If it fails,
    it becomes an oblivion shade spawn under the control
    of the original oblivion shade in 1d4 rounds. An oblivion
    shade spawn usually has a CR that is 3 lower than that
    of the original oblivion shade.
**Void Leap (Su)** An oblivion shade can pass incorporeally
    through the center of a solid object whose space is larger
    than its own, but not an object whose space is larger
    than the distance an oblivion shade can move with a
    single move action (40 feet for most oblivion shades).

A kind of incorporeal undead, an oblivion shade comes into existence when an evil being dies in the throes of utter nihilism. With that negativity burning in its heart, the miserable soul rises again as an oblivion shade.

Oblivion shades are animate expressions of entropy, able to disintegrate matter with a touch. Though their bodies melt away to nearly nothing, victims killed by oblivion shades often find their souls twisted, becoming oblivion shade spawn under the thrall of the original undead.

Most oblivion shades embrace devotion to the Devourer. Some function as soldiers of the Star-Eater's cults, while others act as revered mystics and sages of the most faithful choirs. A few create their own sects by slaughtering innocents to create spawn. These "invisible choirs" are looked upon with fear and awe even by other cultists of the Devourer.

## OBLIVION SHADE TEMPLATE GRAFT (CR 3+)
Oblivion shades are incorporeal undead that appear as flickers at the edge of light. This template can be used to create oblivion shade spawn by simply omitting the create spawn ability.

**Required Creature Type:** Undead.
**Required Subtype:** Incorporeal.
**Traits:** Blindsight (life) 60 ft.; create spawn (see above); set Strength modifier to —; void leap (see above).
**Suggested Ability Score Modifiers:** Dex, Int.

# SCYPHOZOAN

**CR 3**  **XP 800**

Scyphozoan mechanic
N Medium aberration
**Init** +2; **Senses** blindsense (vibration) 30 ft.; **Perception** +8

**DEFENSE**          **HP** 42
**EAC** 14; **KAC** 15
**Fort** +5; **Ref** +5; **Will** +5

**OFFENSE**
**Speed** 30 ft., swim 30 ft.
**Melee** tentacle +7 (1d4+3 A & B)
**Ranged** tactical arc emitter +9 (1d4+3 E)
**Offensive Abilities** overload, target tracking

**STATISTICS**
**Str** +0; **Dex** +2; **Con** +1; **Int** +4; **Wis** +0; **Cha** +0
**Skills** Computers +13, Engineering +13, Life Science +8,
    Medicine +13, Physical Science +8
**Languages** Common, Scyphozoan
**Other Abilities** amphibious, artificial
    intelligence (exocortex),
    custom rig, mechanic tricks
    (energy shield [7 HP,
    3 minutes])
**Gear** scyphozoan bio-weave
(functions as
graphite carbon skin),
tactical arc emitter with 1 battery
(20 charges)

**ECOLOGY**
**Environment** temperate aquatic or
    urban (Primoria)
**Organization** solitary, pair, or
    bloom (3–18)

**SPECIAL ABILITIES**
**Acidic Tentacles (Ex)** As a swift action,
    a scyphozoan can make one of her
    prehensile tentacles secrete acid; her
    unarmed strikes with that tentacle
    count as having the *corrosive* weapon
    fusion, except the ability is not
    magical. While the effect is activated,
    the scyphozoan is considered armed,
    and the attack doesn't
    count as archaic, but the
    scyphozoan cannot
    hold an item in
    that tentacle.

## RACIAL TRAITS

**Ability Adjustments:** +2 Con, +2 Int, –2 Cha
**Hit Points:** 4

**Size and Type:** Scyphozoans are Medium aberrations.
**Acidic Tentacles:** See the stat block.
**Amphibious:** Scyphozoans are able to breathe both
    water and air normally.
**Scyphozoan Senses:** Scyphozoans have blindsense
    (vibration) with a range of 30 feet.
**Sea-Born:** A scyphozoan has a land speed of 30 feet
    and a swim speed of 30 feet.
        **Translucent:** Scyphozoans receive a +2
        racial bonus to Stealth skill checks.

Starting at 3rd level, a scyphozoan
adds 1-1/2 × her character level
to the damage while the effect
is activated. A scyphozoan can
deactivate the effect as a swift action.

Scyphozoans evolved from a species
of large amphibious sea jellies,
which hunted on land
and in water along
the coastlines
of Primoria's
temperate zones
(see page 48). A
scyphozoan has
a soft and translucent body, with
several ambulatory tentacles as well as two
prehensile tentacles. In water, a scyphozoan
swims by expanding and contracting its
bell, which propels the creature forward.
The bell and tentacles are sensitive to
vibrations in the air or water, allowing the
scyphozoan to sense nearby creatures
even if she can't see them. A scyphozoan
is approximately 7 feet tall and weighs
up to 200 pounds. Other species find
it difficult to tell male and female
scyphozoans apart because the
two sexes exhibit few
differing characteristics.

THE
THIRTEENTH
GATE

PART 1:
STATIC SUNS,
CLOCKWORK
PLANETS

PART 2:
COUNTDOWN
TO OBLIVION

PART 3:
LAST GASPS

RELICS OF THE
KISHALEE

ALIEN WORLDS
AND
CULTURES

ALIEN
ARCHIVES

CODEX OF
WORLDS

# SELAMID

NG Medium ooze (selamid)

**Init** +3; **Senses** blindsight (vibration) 60 ft., sightless; **Perception** +18

## DEFENSE      HP 80

**EAC** 18; **KAC** 19

**Fort** +7; **Ref** +3; **Will** +7; +2 vs. gravity effects

**Defensive Abilities** amorphous, gravity adaptation

## OFFENSE

**Speed** 30 ft., climb 20 ft., swim 10 ft.

**Melee** pseudopod +12 (1d6+8 B plus grab)

**Ranged** advanced semi-auto pistol +14 (2d6+6 P)

**Space** 5 ft.; **Reach** 5 ft. (10 ft. with pseudopod)

## STATISTICS

**Str** +2; **Dex** +3; **Con** +5; **Int** +0; **Wis** +1; **Cha** +0

**Skills** Athletics +18, Culture +18, Sense Motive +13, Survival +13

**Languages** Common, Selamidian

**Other Abilities** advanced ooze biology, compression, malleable

**Gear** advanced semi-auto pistol with 12 rounds

## RACIAL TRAITS

**Ability Adjustments:** +2 Dex, +2 Con, –2 Cha

**Hit Points:** 6

**Size and Type:** Selamids are Medium oozes with the selamid subtype, but they do not gain the normal ooze immunities.

**Advanced Ooze Biology:** See the stat block.

**Blindsight:** Selamids have blindsight (vibration) with a range of 60 feet.

**Gravity Adaptation:** See the stat block.

**Malleable:** See the stat block.

**Sightless:** A selamid cannot see and is never subject to any effect that requires it to see a target or effect.

## ECOLOGY

**Environment** any (Silselrik)

**Organization** solitary, pair, work crew (3–12), or community (50+ plus 50% noncombatants)

## SPECIAL ABILITIES

**Advanced Ooze Biology (Ex)** Selamids are not immune to critical hits, are not mindless, and can gain and use skills normally. For effects targeting creatures by type, selamids count as both humanoids and oozes (whichever type allows an ability to affect them for abilities that affect only one type, and whichever is worse for abilities that affect both creature types).

**Gravity Adaptation (Ex)** Selamids can always take 10 on Athletics checks in zero gravity.

**Malleable (Ex)** A selamid can manipulate and wear equipment as a creature with two arms, and equipment and armor of the appropriate size never needs to be adjusted to allow the selamid to use it. It gains a +8 racial bonus to Acrobatics checks to escape.

Adapted to survive in fluctuating gravity, selamids are creatures of complex, flexible protoplasm. Though selamids can eat nearly any organic matter, their diets usually consist of material sloughed from other oozes on their home world (see page 52). At the end of its 40-year life span, a selamid divides to "birth" new selamids.

# SEPREVOI

**CR 3** | **XP 800**

LN Medium monstrous humanoid (seprevoi)
**Init** +4; **Senses** darkvision 60 ft.; **Perception** +13

## DEFENSE                                           HP 35
**EAC** 14; **KAC** 15
**Fort** +4, **Ref** +4, **Will** +6; +2 vs. radiation, –2 vs. disease
**Defensive Abilities** multi-legged, orbital adaptation
**Weaknesses** vulnerable to disease

## OFFENSE
**Speed** 40 ft.
**Melee** tactical dueling sword +9 (1d6+4 S)
**Ranged** autotarget rifle +11 (1d6+3 P)
**Offensive Abilities** analog attunement

## STATISTICS
**Str** +1; **Dex** +4; **Con** +0; **Int** –1; **Wis** +0; **Cha** +2
**Skills** Acrobatics +13, Culture +8, Diplomacy +8,
Sense Motive +13
**Languages** Seprevoi

## SPECIAL ABILITIES
**Analog Attunement (Ex)** A seprevoi using a weapon with
the analog or archaic weapon property receives a
+1 racial bonus on attack rolls, due to
the centuries of rationing
that restricted the race's
access to and familiarity
with powered or otherwise
advanced technology.

**Multi-Legged (Ex)** Seprevois have four legs, which
makes them particularly stable in areas of normal or
higher gravity. A seprevois gains a +2 bonus to its KAC
against combat maneuvers to trip or move it from its
position.

**Orbital Adaptation (Ex)** Most seprevois live their whole
lives in zero-g environments in the spacecraft orbiting
their home world. While a seprevoi must still attempt
all required skill checks to move in zero-g, failure at
any such checks never imparts the off-kilter condition
to the creature. Additionally, seprevois have a natural
resistance to radiation. A seprevoi gains a +2 bonus
to saving throws to resist radiation and radiation
sickness (*Starfinder Core Rulebook* 404). Finally,
seprevois have weakened immune systems, such
that they take a –2 penalty to saving throws against
diseases (except radiation sickness).

Seprevois evolved from the simian creatures of their home
world (see page 50). They are covered in fine, short hair
ranging in color from dark brown to pale blond, except for
the black skin of their faces and hands. Seprevois have
six elongated fingers on each hand, each featuring an
additional joint compared to a human's hand.
Seprevois' four feet have three unjointed toes each.

## RACIAL TRAITS

**Ability Adjustments:** +2 Dex, +2 Cha, –2 Int
**Hit Points:** 6

**Size and Type:** Seprevois are Medium monstrous
humanoids with the seprevoi subtype.
**Analog Attunement:** See the stat block.
**Fast:** Seprevois have a land speed of 40 feet.
**Multi-Legged:** See the stat block.
**Orbital Adaptation:** See the stat block.

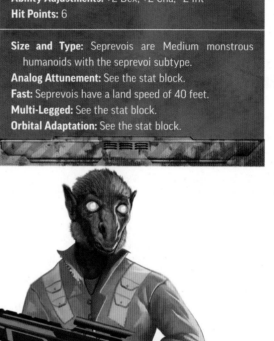

THE
THIRTEENTH
GATE

PART 1:
STATIC SUNS,
CLOCKWORK
PLANETS

PART 2:
COUNTDOWN
TO OBLIVION

PART 3:
LAST GASPS

RELICS OF THE
KISHALEE

ALIEN WORLDS
AND
CULTURES

ALIEN
ARCHIVES

CODEX OF
WORLDS

## URRAKAR

*Cold World of Shadows and Black Emeralds*

**Diameter:** ×2/3; **Mass:** ×1/2
**Gravity:** ×1
**Location:** The Vast
**Atmosphere:** Thick
**Day:** 12 hours; **Year:** 412 years

Urrakar is the lone planet of the Urran system, which is composed mostly of asteroid belts and dense cloud rings. The location of the Urran system appeared on numerous Pact Worlds and Veskarium planetary infospheres almost simultaneously, shortly after devotees of Triune visited it as they were spreading Drift beacons throughout the galaxy. No one has stepped forward to claim responsibility for disseminating the information, and even those priests who first encountered the area claim to have had no hand in this strange occurrence. Despite the mystery surrounding Urrakar, many groups in the Pact Worlds have begun exploring the planet's surface and exploiting its natural resources.

Urrakar is even farther from its star than Aucturn is from the Pact Worlds' sun, which places the planet well outside what would normally be the system's habitable zone (where water can exist in a liquid state on a planet's surface). However, Urrakar's extremely dense composition helps keep the planet's core molten. This, combined with tidal heating and the radioactive decay of its heaviest elements, allows Urrakar to maintain a surface temperature just above water's freezing point. The planet also has a strong magnetic field, which protects it from cosmic rays despite its great range from the solar winds of its star.

The constant churning of molten metals within Urrakar's core makes the planet very active volcanically, with gases constantly spewing from hot springs, massive cinder cones, and vents. As such, the planet has a dense atmosphere with a strong metallic odor. The air is sometimes thick with ash, and while the trace chemicals found in the atmosphere aren't in high enough concentrations to qualify as toxic, long-term exposure without protection is likely to damage the lungs of most non-native air-breathing creatures.

Urrakar is a dark, cold world. Even at noon, its sun is nothing more than a point in the sky, dimmer than a full moon and safe to look at with the naked eye. Otherwise, it's lit only by the glow of lava below jagged mountains from strong tectonic activity, the planet is veiled in huge, dense shadows. The darkest of these areas have weak connections to the Shadow Plane, through which creatures from that plane can sometimes pass. Urrakar has no native fauna, but umbral versions of many creatures from throughout the galaxy can be found across the world, often hunting smaller shadowy creatures and anything else they can track and potentially consume.

The combination of energy from the Shadow Plane and heavy metals also causes Urrakar to be the only known source of black emeralds—gemstones infused with innate magic potential. Black emeralds are valuable resources for the manufacture of spell gems that hold necromantic magic and some forms of *solarian weapon crystals*. Several companies, most notably Arabani Arms, Ltd. and Ulrikka Clanholdings, have small mining operations on the planet that focus on extracting black emeralds. Usually consisting of a single heated and pressurized prefab building, these mining facilities are generally separated by hundreds of miles with little but empty plains between them. Direct competition for resources between these enterprises is currently rare, as the stripping of Urrakar's gem fields has only just begun. However, a few conglomerates (such as Astral Extractions) have begun to engage in underhanded tactics and corporate sabotage to gain the upper hand.

# NEXT MONTH

## EMPIRE OF BONES

*By Owen K.C. Stephens*

The undead Corpse Fleet has appeared within the strange star system known as the Gate of Twelve Suns, intent on seizing the ancient alien superweapon called the Stellar Degenerator. The heroes are massively outgunned, and their only hope lies in infiltrating the fleet's flagship and seizing control of the vessel's bridge. Only then can they set the ship to self-destruct and pilot it on a collision course with the superweapon. If they succeed, the heroes can obliterate the Stellar Degenerator and render the galaxy safe once again, but they'll need to escape the destruction to live to tell the tale!

## CONTINUING THE CAMPAIGN

*By John Compton*

The heroes have destroyed the Stellar Degenerator, but their adventures don't have to end there! From dealing with a powerful extraplanar entity summoned upon opening the superweapon's demiplane to battling more servants of the Devourer, this article is chock full of plot hooks and ideas for any Dead Suns campaign to continue on.

## SHIPS OF THE LINE

*By Owen K.C. Stephens*

Sometimes battleships and dreadnoughts just aren't big enough! This article presents new rules for starships of extraordinary size and power capable of acting as mobile bases for entire fleets.

## SHIPS OF THE CORPSE FLEET

*By Jason Keeley*

The exiled undead navy known as the Corpse Fleet shows no signs of ceasing its activities. Discover new starship options for expansion bays and weapons, and witness the might of several new Corpse Fleet vessels of various tiers!

## SUBSCRIBE TO STARFINDER ADVENTURE PATH

The Dead Suns Adventure Path concludes! Don't miss out on a single exciting volume—head over to **paizo.com/starfinder** and subscribe today to have Starfinder Roleplaying Game, Starfinder Adventure Path, and Starfinder Accessories products delivered to your door!

TEMPLE OF THE TWELVE

PART 1: STATIC SUNS, CLOCKWORK PLANETS

PART 2: COUNTDOWN TO OBLIVION

PART 3: LAST GASPS

RELICS OF THE KISHALEE

ALIEN WORLDS AND CULTURES

ALIEN ARCHIVES

CODEX OF WORLDS

# BRAVE NEW WORLDS!

# STARFINDER®

# PACT WORLDS

Experience the wonders of the Pact Worlds in this definitive, 216-page hardcover campaign setting for the Starfinder Roleplaying Game! The book contains detailed gazetteers for all worlds of the Absalom Pact, as well as new character themes for each Pact World. Travel the galaxy with the starships of Aballon, Verces, the Hellknights, the Iomedaeans, and the Xenowardens, or play as a member of one of six new alien races: shapechanging astrazoans, rolling bantrids, undead borais, plantlike khizars, robotic SROs, or winged strix. With tons of new archetypes, feats, spells, equipment, and NPC stat blocks, *Starfinder Pact Worlds* reveals the secrets and mysteries of the solar system and its inhabitants in all their science fantasy glory!

# AVAILABLE NOW!